# VINTAGE
# PARTY
# GAMES

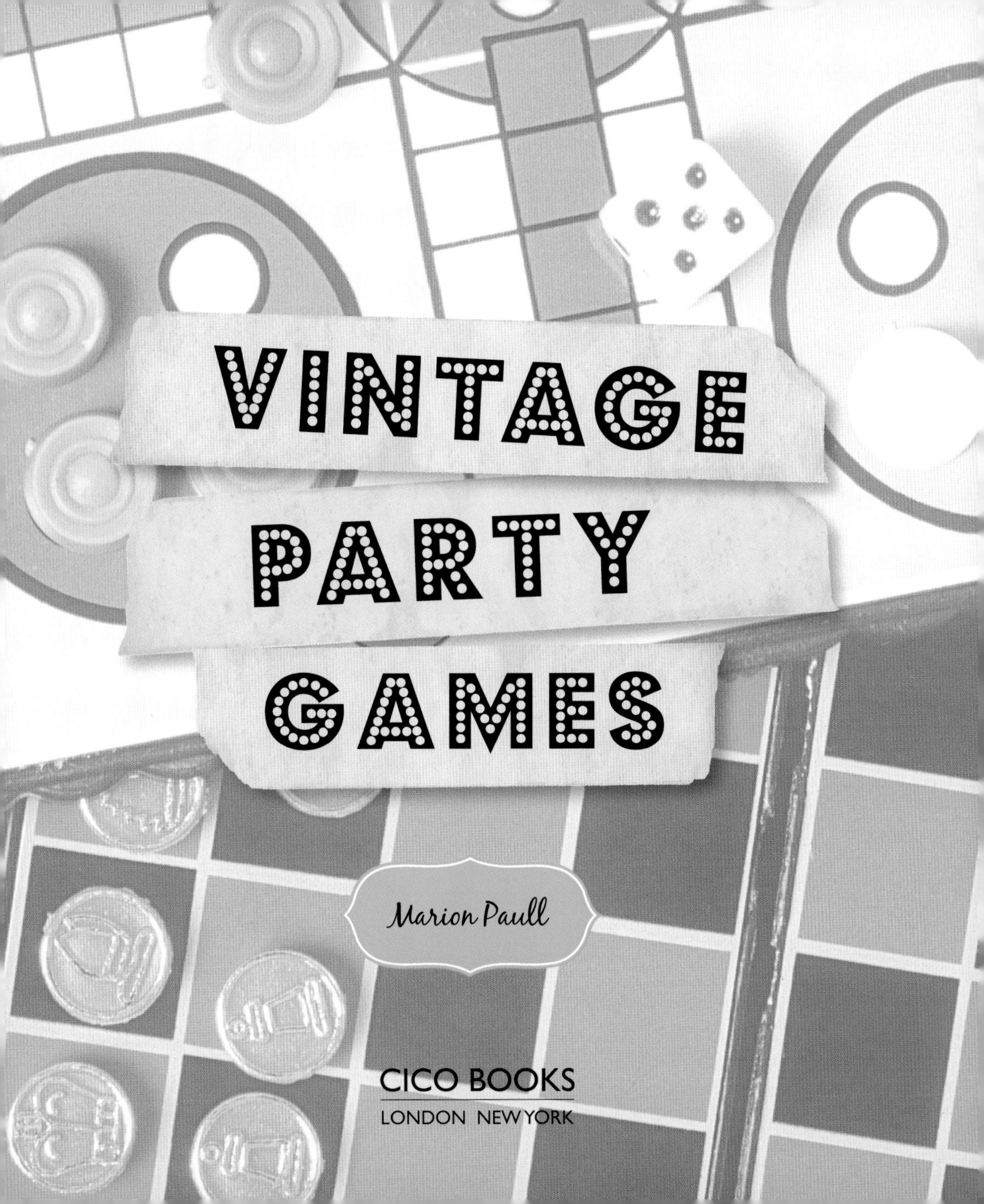

# VINTAGE PARTY GAMES

Marion Paull

**CICO BOOKS**

LONDON  NEW YORK

Published in 2015 by CICO Books

An imprint of Ryland Peters & Small Ltd

20–21 Jockey's Fields
341 E 116th St

London WC1R 4BW
New York, NY 10029

www.rylandpeters.com

10 9 8 7 6 5 4 3 2 1

Text © Marion Paull 2015

Design and illustrations by Alice Potter
on pages 1, 2, 10, 18, 19, 21, 30, 35, 41,
44, 49, 50, 54, 64, 66, 70, 73, 75, 80, 84,
94, 98, 103, and 122 © CICO Books 2015

All other illustrations and photographs
© Corbis

A CIP catalog record for this book is
available from the Library of Congress
and the British Library.

ISBN: 978 1 78249 258 0

Printed in China

Designer: Mark Latter

Illustrator: Alice Potter

In-house editor: Anna Galkina

Art director: Sally Powell

Head of production: Patricia Harrington

Publishing manager: Penny Craig

Publisher: Cindy Richards

# CONTENTS

Introduction **6**

**Chapter 1:**
## PLAYTIME BEFORE COMPUTERS **10**
Retro playthings **16**
Make believe **22**
Counting out **24**
Forfeits **28**

**Chapter 2:**
## PLAYING OUTSIDE **30**
Outdoor amusements **33**
Chasing games **50**
Ball games **62**

**Chapter 3:**
## PARTY TIME **70**
Rings and arches **74**
Sneaking up and "do as I do" **84**
Search and try to find **88**
Games you can't ignore **92**

**Chapter 4:**
## PARLOR GAMES **98**
Guessing games **102**
Word games **110**
Tabletop games **120**
Board games **128**

Resources **140**
Index **142**
Acknowledgments **144**

# INTRODUCTION

What is a game? That may seem a simple question but many philosophers, intellectuals, and other deep-thinkers since Wittgenstein, and probably earlier, have tried to come up with the definitive answer and each one is different (and often fairly incomprehensible). Narrowing it down to children's games doesn't help that much. They can be structured or unstructured, use toys or equipment or not, be played indoors or out, involve skill or luck (or both), be played alone or by a group, in cooperation or competitively, involve strategic thinking or not, and probably a whole raft of other things too.

> "There is nothing in the the world so irresistibly contagious as laughter and good humor."
>
> Charles Dickens,
> *A Christmas Carol* (1843)

> "Children need the freedom and time to play. Play is not a luxury. Play is a necessity."
>
> Kay Redfield Jamison, clinical psychologist and writer

And what about their purpose? Apparently, games are there to entertain, to educate, as therapy, to provide exercise, and to help develop moral judgment and the ability to understand and obey rules. Although no one would argue with any of that, it all seems a bit much to load on to childish shoulders. As a non-academic, it seems to me that the fundamental reason why kids play games is to have fun and shouldn't that be their main purpose? And how about just running around letting off steam!

"Some day you will be old enough to read fairy tales again."

C.S. Lewis (1898–1963), author and scholar

> "We don't stop playing because we grow old; we grow old because we stop playing."
>
> George Bernard Shaw (1856–1950), playwright and critic

So any attempt to classify children's games, traditional or not, presents something of a conundrum, given that they are such a mix and constantly evolving. I've divided them in a way that seems logical to me but is necessarily fairly arbitrary. There is no reason at all why Hide and Seek, for example, can't be played at recess (school break time) or on any weekend, indoors or out, when a group of kids gets together—no need to wait for someone to have a party! When it comes to where and when to play, there are no hard and fast rules.

One thing is certain, however—*homo sapiens* love to play games and that starts in childhood. When following in the game-playing footsteps of our forebears, we are spoilt for choice. Those activities described here are just a few among hundreds, possibly thousands. Some will be familiar, others less so. It would be a shame if any are forgotten, not just for reasons of nostalgia and continuity, and not just for their undoubted educational and sociological advantages, but because they give everyone a good time.

These are old-fashioned children's games, but that doesn't mean you have to be a child to play them! There's no upper age restriction. You can introduce them to your kids or grandkids and leave them to it, or you can join in. And for all those who are big kids at heart, you can sneak in a game or two—maybe of the less strenuous variety—with likeminded friends, even when no kids are around. Why not? I for one have no wish to put away childish things—well, not entirely anyway. As Walt Disney is reputed to have said, "That's the real trouble with the world, too many people grow up." So please bear with me if in some instructions I've referred to "you" rather than "them," meaning the children (rather given myself away!). Also, in the old days, games were much more likely to be regarded as gender specific—not so now, I'm pleased to say, so in the instructions "he" and "she" are used indiscriminately. These games are for everyone who wants to take part.

Chapter 1

# PLAYTIME BEFORE COMPUTERS

Children have always played games. Boys and girls probably chased each other in and out of their home caves in a prehistoric version of Tag, and squeezed into unlikely places, waiting to be found in a primitive game of Hide and Seek.

Some would have us believe that all games have evolved from a core of three or four, which were based on religious rites or cultural practices. Whether that's the case or not, it's certainly true that, over the centuries, games have developed and spread across the world through trade, exploration, and mass migration, changing a lot or a little along the way. Remarkably, some games remain more or less the same—children playing marbles today are not so different from the youth of ancient Greece, who were doing much the same thing using polished nuts rather than glass balls. How to play may vary, though. You can find different versions of hopscotch, for instance, being played in India, Russia, Brazil, Australia, and all the countries of Europe as well as in America and Britain.

"I used my imagination to make the grass whatever color I wanted it to be."

Whoopi Goldberg,
actress and TV presenter

"There are no blueprints for couch cushion forts."

Dee Ann Stewart,
*What Spock Forgot*
(2003)

These games, inherited and much loved by our parents, grandparents, and great grandparents, will undoubtedly survive for generations to come, but others, or specific versions of them, are in danger of being overlooked, lost even, in these high-tech, digital days of online wonders. Gaming has taken on a whole new meaning. Online games are fast, exciting, sophisticated, and available at the press of a button, or a strategic click. They hone quick-thinking and fast reactions and kids love them. These are children of the computer age and you'll never totally prise them away from all, or any, of the screens that have become an integral part of their lives, nor should you try.

However, valuable as screen time is, playtime away from it is equally, if not more, important. Comes a time when the joy of running about in the fresh air, letting off steam in the great outdoors, playing with pals—real ones, face to face, not avatars—in a structured or unstructured way is irresistible, even now. For a child, a game devised around jumping in puddles can be laugh-out-loud fun, and that's the key. Kids love playing because it's fun. An electronic device is just a tool they use in

> "Just play. Have fun. Enjoy the game."
>
> Michael Jordan, professional basketball player

> "Children are never more serious than when they play."
>
> Michel de Montaigne, *Essays* (1580)

pursuit of that admirable aim, and there are hundreds of others in the shape of toys.

However, the best tool available to kids intent on having fun is their imagination. Constructing a den or hideaway out of anything to hand, and making up all sorts of

scenarios to act out is an all-consuming business, and no less enjoyable for that. Ideas flow naturally, the children encouraging each other and taking it so seriously. Games of Cops and Robbers or Cowboys and Indians may seem outdated, but these old-fashioned notions take on a modern slant in the hearts and minds of the most technically savvy kids, just as they did in the old days.

That was when, in the absence of tablets, iphones, laptops and even televisions, children spent a lot of time in the company of other kids, inventing all sorts of different ways to play every game they had ever come across. If any equipment was needed, they used what they could find—sticks, stones, pebbles, buttons, tin cans, chalk to draw lines on the ground. Necessity, in the eyes of the child, was the mother of invention. In Victorian times, rich kids had bought toys; children of poorer families improvised. Their parents would improvise, too, making them clothes-peg dolls, rag balls, paper windmills and, if they were lucky, whittled wooden figures.

Those games of yesteryear are just as much fun today as they always were, and deserve a revival, whether played to the old rules or adapted to the times, as children have always done. What were street games can be played in backyards, schoolyards, and playgrounds, or out in the woods and fields of the countryside— and even in the streets still, if traffic-free.

# RETRO PLAYTHINGS

Many of the toys familiar to our great grandparents' generation are still popular today, while others have fallen out of fashion. You don't see many boys or girls happily galloping along on their hobby horses these days, or watching a zoetrope in enthralled admiration. Pogo sticks, on the other hand, have caught the imaginations of a new set of young thrill-seekers and, unlikely as it may seem, entered the realms of extreme sports.

Those old toys that are still around, albeit in modern guise, have lost none of their power to engross and entertain, and are doubtless not thought of as old-fashioned. Jigsaw puzzles, painting by numbers, blowing soap bubbles, roller skates, kick scooters, Jacob's ladder, and solitaire are examples of oldies that have been given a makeover, while dolls, marionette puppets, and glove puppets are universal and have never gone out of style. Others, such as the hula hoop and space hopper, are not so old, but probably old enough to be thought of as retro by today's kids.

PLAYTIME BEFORE COMPUTERS

"To drive a top was my delight
From early morning until night;
Or to blow, single or double,
Through a tube a bright soap-bubble,
Or a batch of three or four,
To rejoice our eyes the more."

Jean Froissart (c1337–c1405),
poet and chronicler of his times

17

# Hoop and stick

In the Victorian era, you couldn't walk along a street without the danger of being accosted by a series of hoops, iron or wooden, skillfully propelled along with alarming speed by a succession of small children, intent on beating each other to some designated spot, or directing their hoops between two stones (or something similar) without touching or mishap. Trundling, it was called, or rolling, and it has been popular all over the world since the days of ancient Greece. Wooden hoops were struck with a stick, and iron hoops with an iron rod, hooked at one end, with a wooden handle. Now you seldom see children playing with a hoop and stick, but you can still find wooden ones to buy and, given enough space, kids could still have fun with them.

PLAYTIME BEFORE COMPUTERS

# Old-fashioned toys

Many traditional toys, quite a few of which have ancient origins, are enjoying a resurgence of popularity. Here are just a few—parents and grandparents can probably think of many more:

- Automata and mechanical toys
- Bagatelle
- Clockwork toys
- Diabolo
- Dinky toys
- Humming top
- Kaleidoscope
- Kite
- Meccano
- Modeling clay
- Quoits/ring toss
- Rocking horse
- Skittles
- Stilts
- Tin noisemakers
- Whip and top
- Wooden cup and ball
- Yo-yo

# Five Stones

You can't get a much more descriptive name for a toy than this! Knucklebones is another name for it, which was just as descriptive in its day. In ancient Greece and Rome, the knuckle bones of sheep and goats were used and the name, as well as the games, survived at least into the 20th century. Dabs, dibs, chuck-stones, and jacks are other names for more or less the same thing. Jacks were made of metal and six-pronged. There were often ten of them and you played with a particularly bouncy rubber ball. You can still buy jacks, although they are usually made of plastic (including the ball).

As a child, if I'd forgotten to take my dabs to the beach, I'd just search for five small, smooth pebbles and clear a spot on the beach towel to play on, or, even better, find a flat rock (still do!). Several children can take turns to play with the same set, passing on the stones each time a maneuver fails to come off. The games devised to play with this wondrous toy are many and varied, and present marvelous tests of dexterity. Here are a few of the old ones.

✳ Throw up one stone and catch it on the back of your hand. Toss it up in the air and catch it in the palm of the same hand. Do the same again with two stones, then three, four, and five.

✳ Throw up all the stones and catch as many as you can on the back of your hand. Toss them back up in the air and catch as many as you can. You're often left with just one by this stage (or none, in which case it's time for the next person to have a turn). Throw it in the air and, with the same hand, pick up one stone left on the ground. Carry on until you've picked up all the stones.

✳ Roll the stones out all at once. Select one, throw it up, and pick up the rest one at a time with the same hand. As you pick up each stone, keep it in your hand while you throw up your master stone to collect another from the ground. Alternatively, each time, throw up all the stones in your hand to collect those remaining, one at a time—so, if you get this far, you'll be throwing up four to pick up the last one.

✳ Throw up one stone and catch it on the back of your hand. Keep it there while you collect all the others between the splayed fingers of the same hand. Toss up the now wobbling stone, quickly turn over your hand, still clasping the rest between your fingers, and catch it in that palm. Then maneuver the stones from between your fingers to join the stone in your palm. (Hard enough with dabs, practically impossible with pebbles!)

# Teddy bears

It's hard to imagine a time without teddy bears but, in fact, they were first made in the early part of the twentieth century. The clue's in the name—they were called teddy bears after Theodore "Teddy" Roosevelt. The story goes that on a bear-hunting trip in Mississippi, Roosevelt refused to shoot a bear that had been captured and set up for him as a target—a great story for a political cartoon in the *Washington Post*. Toymakers Morris and Rose Michtom saw the cartoon, spotted an opportunity, and received presidential permission to call the resulting soft toy "Teddy's bear."

At the same time, in one of those inexplicable coincidences, German toymakers Steiff had also come up with the idea of a soft-toy bear cub with jointed limbs. Richard Steiff, the founder's nephew, spent hours at the local zoo, studying and drawing the bears there, and he created the designs himself. Both the Michtom and Steiff bears were unveiled in early 1903, and in 1904, Steiff bears were the big hit of the World's Fair in Saint Louis, picking up the gold medal. Nowadays, if you come across a Steiff bear, identifiable by a metal tag in its ear, you could be into serious money!

# MAKE BELIEVE

Before the electronic age, children loved their toys, especially if they didn't have many of them, and they weaved these precious objects into imaginative games of make believe. Tin or wooden soldiers and miniature tea sets were carefully stored and brought out when the opportunity arose for pretend battles or dollies' tea parties. The lucky ones might have a tin pedal car to zoom around in, or a tricycle. Toy theaters were particularly popular, as were paper characters with costumes you could change with foldover tabs, and cardboard accessories to assemble yourself. Just imagine what plays and entertainments the kids conjured up! You can still buy vintage-style, cut-out figures to make up—jointed, too!

# Classic games with babies and toddlers

Nursery rhymes, singsongs, and rounds are all a delight to the very young, and many of those that brought a smile to the chubby cheeks of our parents and grandparents are doing the same for little ones today. Fingerplays are usually an especially big hit. How many times have the little piggies gone to market and how often has incy wincy spider been rained off only to return triumphant?

Once the babies get a little older, they (mostly!) love to play familiar singing games with other toddlers—"Row, Row, Row your Boat," "Here we go round the Mulberry Bush," and "See Saw Marjory Daw" never seem to lose their charm. And what about trying "The Grand Old Duke of York," "The Galloping Major," and that old favorite, "One, Two, Buckle My Shoe?" Fun unlimited!

"Imagination is more important than knowledge."

Albert Einstein (1879–1955), theoretical physicist and philosopher

# COUNTING OUT

How to decide who is going to be "It," the chaser, hider, or one whose role is different from everybody else's? Aside from choosing which hand holds the pebble, or tossing a coin, which decide between two only, an age-old method is to use a set rhyme, or what could be loosely described as such. This is the equivalent of casting lots, and although possibly not as old as that, counting-out rhymes, or dips, have apparently been in existence for centuries, and in more or less the same form all over the world. Most of the old rhymes are meaningless now, and usually include a fair number of nonsense words. Their origins must be fascinating (but beyond the scope of this book).

"We may be tolerably sure that Shakespeare and Sidney directed their childish sports by the very same rhymes which are still employed for the purpose."

William Newell Games and Songs of American Children (1884)

# How dips work

Someone (often self-selected) does the counting by reciting the rhyme and at each syllable pointing at each player in turn, including himself. Whoever is being indicated at the end stands aside. Somehow, it never seems to be the one doing the counting! Players can be counted out by these means, so It is the last one left, or counted in, so It is the one at the wrong end of the pointing finger first time. Decide which it's to be before dipping begins.

An exception to the usual pointing routine was One Potato. Everyone lined up with their two fists held out in front. The one doing the counting came along and tapped each fist with his own, saying, "One potato, two potato, three potato, four; five potato, six potato, seven potato, more." The "more" fist's owner withdrew it behind his back and the counting went on in the same way until only one fist was left held out in front. It had been chosen; let the game commence.

Ena, deena, dina, dust
Catler, wheeler, whiler, whust
Spin, spon, must be done
Twiddleum, twaddleum, twenty-one.

"I like nonsense; it wakes up the brain cells."

Dr Seuss (1904–1991), author and cartoonist

Hoky poky, winky, wum
How do you like your 'taters done?
Snip, snap, snorum
High popolorum
Kate go scratch it
You are out!

Eeny, meeny, mackeracka
Air, aye, dominacka
Chickapoppa, Lollipoppa
Om, pom, push.

Dip, dip, dip
My little ship
Sailing on the water
Like a cup and saucer
The one who comes to number three
Shall surely be out
One, two three.

27

# FORFEITS

"It may be the games are silly, but then so are human beings."

Robert Lynd (1879–1949),
writer and essayist

As a game in its own right, Forfeits was popular in Victorian times. Someone was sent out of sight while everyone else put a small item into a communal box or bowl. The judge came back, picked out each item in turn, and gave its owner something silly to do in order to reclaim it.

However, forfeits are perhaps better known as the price to pay for making a mistake in another game—same silliness, different circumstance, although Alice Bertha Gomme, in *The Traditional Games of England, Scotland and Ireland* (1894), suggests that the paying of forfeits was very similar to the game. Everyone incurring a forfeit put a small item in the box and was obliged to redeem it when the game came to an end. Forfeits were "'cried' in the following manner. One of the players sits on a chair having the forfeits in her lap. A child kneels on the ground and buries his face in his hands on the lap of the person who holds the forfeits. The 'crier' then takes up indiscriminately one of the forfeits, and holding it up in the sight of all those who have been playing the games (without the kneeling child seeing it), says—

'Here's a very pretty thing and a very pretty thing,
And what shall be done to [or, by] the owner of this very pretty thing?'

The kneeling child then says what the penance is to be. The owner of the forfeit must then perform the penance before the other players, and then another forfeit is 'cried.'"

You can still play in the old-fashioned way, but perhaps decide what penances to choose from beforehand, so there are no nasty surprises and no one is upset at what they are asked to do. They can be anything you like within reason—singing a song, walking around the room backward, standing on a chair and shouting, "I am an idiot!", pretending to walk a tightrope, anything at all, but perhaps tailor them to the participants in the game.

# Victorian forfeits

According to Alice Bertha Gomme, the following were among the "more general penances imposed upon the owners of the forfeits":

➤ Kneel to the prettiest, bow to the wittiest, and kiss the one you love best.

➤ Stand in each corner of the room—sigh in one, cry in another, sing in another, and dance in the other.

➤ Place two chairs in the middle of the room, take off your shoes, and jump over them.

➤ Measure so many yards of love ribbon.

➤ Spell "Opportunity."

Lady Gomme also lists biting an inch off the poker and crawling up the chimney—a bit much for anyone, let alone children in their party clothes! She also includes putting yourself through the keyhole—I do wonder how you were supposed to do that! Spelling "Opportunity" seems a doddle in comparison—and what's love ribbon?

Chapter 2

# PLAYING

## OUTSIDE

These days, for safety's sake, playing outside means in backyards, parks, schoolyards, and playgrounds, often under the supervision of an adult. In the old days, however, when traffic was not so fast or frequent, especially in cities where grassy spaces were few and far between, playing outside meant playing in the street with the rest of the neighborhood kids.

A whole street culture developed among children, and children being as inventive then as they ever were, that included a multitude of games. Ideas for the games may have been universal—chasing, hiding, competing—but locally the kids made their own rules to suit, and so the same game varied in detail from town to town, even from neighborhood to neighborhood. If any tool was needed, kids used whatever came to hand—sticks, stones, pieces of wood, old washing lines for skipping ropes, tin cans, conkers.

Many of these games can still be played—no expensive equipment required—and are just as much fun now as they were when our grandparents, and great grandparents, dreamed them up all those years ago.

"It is a happy talent to know how to play."

Ralph Waldo Emerson (1803–1882), poet, essayist, and philosopher

# OUTDOOR AMUSEMENTS

If children don't feel like running around in an overly energetic Tag game, there's no need for them to be at a loose end out in the fresh air. A whole array of simple games may claim their attention, activities that can take five minutes or go on all afternoon. The gentle Pooh Sticks is a wonderful entertainment for all ages—dropping sticks in a flowing stream on one side of a bridge and crossing to watch them emerge on the other side. Which one is first—can you remember which one is yours? If streams are noticeable by their absence, refresh memories of how the game was invented by delving into *The House at Pooh Corner*.

# Simple pleasures

The knotty problem of Cat's Cradle is there to be solved all over again by succeeding generations. Kick the Wickey consists of someone kicking a foot-long (30 centimeter) stick and playmates trying to catch it. You can't get much simpler than that, and if it palls after a while, what about Leapfrog or Tug-o'-War—when did these two oldies go out of style?

A line of kids holding hands like the spoke in a wheel and attempting to run in a circle always finds a fair share of volunteers. The one in the middle moves slowly while all along the line the children have to go faster and faster until the ones on the end go flying off. Crack the Whip they used to call it, guaranteed to raise a smile, especially among spectators.

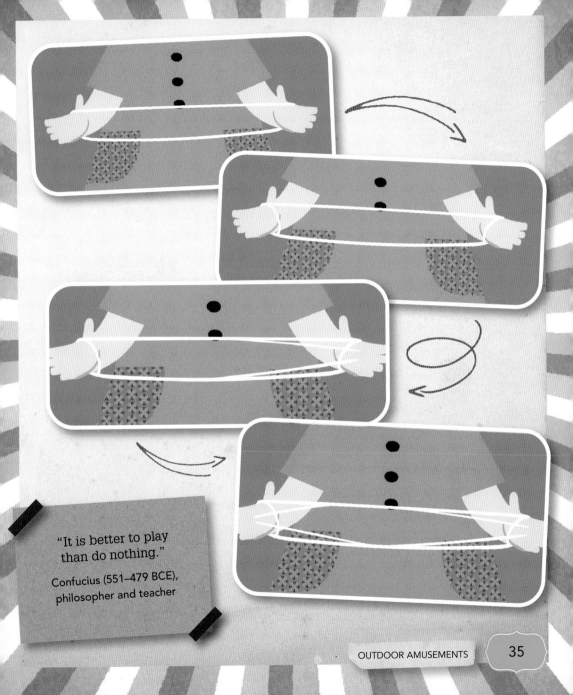

"It is better to play than do nothing."

Confucius (551–479 BCE), philosopher and teacher

# Buttons

At its simplest, players attempt to pitch two buttons into a prepared hole in the ground from a few yards away. A slightly more complicated version has the hole, about the size of a teacup, near a wall or tree, and up to ten buttons being pitched at the same time. In the unlikely event of all of them finding the hole, the pitcher wins the game. Usually, several end up on the ground and the non-player(s) select the most awkwardly positioned for the pitcher to attack with what in the old days was called a "nicker"—a heavy, round counter of some sort. By throwing the nicker, the pitcher tries to knock the chosen button into the hole. Only this will do. If he misses or knocks another button into the hole, or his nicker falls in accidentally, he loses.

In New York, according to William Newell in *Songs and Games of American Children* (1884), all the players toss their buttons toward the hole from about four yards (three or four meters) away, "and whoever comes nearest the hole has the first shot. He endeavors to drive the buttons of the rest into the hole, striking them with the extended thumb by a movement of the whole hand, which is kept flat and stiff. When he misses, the next takes his turn, and so on. Whoever drives the adversary's button into the hole wins it." Who needs a nicker when a thumb will do?

## Skyte the Bob

This Scottish game involves at least two or three players placing a button each on a flat stone called the "bob." From behind a line a few yards away, the players take it in turns to throw a small stone, the "pitcher," at the bob. Any buttons that fall off and land nearer to the pitcher than to the bob may be claimed by the thrower. Any that are knocked nearer to another pitcher may be taken by that stone's owner. If three play and at the end of a round one of them has two buttons, Billy Nobuttons goes first in the next round.

# Skipping

These days jumping rope has come of age as an international sport with its own rules and regulations and governing bodies. A hundred or so years ago things were different. Skipping was either a training aid or, more often, a jolly playtime activity beloved of many kids. If you had your own skipping rope, you could even play by yourself; with a longer rope, you needed at least two others—two to turn the rope, one to skip. If you had your own, beside straight skipping, you could try jumping high enough and turning the rope fast enough for it to go around twice before your feet touched the ground again—that was the "bumps"; or you could cross your arms while still turning the rope—that was "Cross-overs"; or a friend could jump in and skip with you, and then jump out again to allow another friend in, if there were several of you—that was "Visiting." Given a long rope, kids devised plenty of other variations to practice. A few are listed here—why not give them a go? Unless everyone's very good, it won't be long before the rope becomes entangled in feet and legs and you have to start over again.

* **Pepper, Salt, Mustard, Cider, Vinegar.** The rope turners recite this chant, slowly at first and then progressively faster, turning the rope in time, until the skipper trips or runs out of steam.

* **Chase the Fox.** The first skipper, or fox, runs under the rope as it's being turned toward her and all the others follow. Then she runs back under the rope. Then she runs in, skips once, and runs out again; then twice, and so on. Each time the others follow suit until someone messes up. That person changes places with one of the rope turners and they start again.

* **Begging (or Pass the Baker).** Two run in and skip together, first side by side and then changing places. As they do so, one says, "Give me some bread and butter," and the other replies, "Try my next door neighbor."

* **Baking Bread.** One runs in carrying a stone or some other small object, which she repeatedly puts down on the ground and picks up again while still skipping.

* **Rock the Cradle.** In this one, the turners in effect become swingers—swinging the rope from side to side rather than turning it right over.

## Skipping rhymes

These were many and various, chanted by the rope turners and probably everyone else waiting for their turn. Here are just a few to try.

Apples, pears, peaches, plums

Tell me when your birthday comes

January, February, March …

When it comes to the months, the rope turners turn very fast indeed until the skipper shouts, "Yes," and jumps out. Born in December? Unlucky!

Every morning at eight o'clock,

You all may hear the postman's knock.

One, two, three, four.

There goes "Sally."

Whoever is named jumps out while at the same time the next in line jumps in.

Teddy Bear, Teddy Bear, turn around

Teddy Bear, Teddy Bear, touch the ground

Teddy Bear, Teddy Bear, show your shoe

Teddy Bear, Teddy Bear, that will do!

Teddy Bear, Teddy Bear, go upstairs

Teddy Bear, Teddy Bear, say your prayers

Teddy Bear, Teddy Bear, turn out the light

Teddy Bear, Teddy Bear, say goodnight!

The skipper must perform all the actions without missing a jump.

# The Game of Graces

A gentle game for two people that originated in nineteenth century France, it was supposed to encourage gracefulness and so, at one time, girls were encouraged to play it. Perhaps it was invented by a bored young lady, who thought up the gracefulness theory as a good excuse to abandon her embroidery in favor of a little more fun in the great outdoors. Anyway, there's no reason why boys should be excluded.

Equipment needed is two wooden dowels, or sticks, per player and a wooden hoop, usually decorated with ribbons (these days, the hoop is more likely to be plastic, but wood is old-style). The two players stand roughly 15 feet (4.5 meters) or so apart. One player threads the hoop on to her sticks and crosses them into an X shape, tilting them upward slightly. Then with a forward motion, she quickly pushes the sticks apart to send the hoop flying across to player number two, who catches it on her sticks and returns it in similar fashion. You can score, if you like, by starting with an agreed number of points each and deducting one for a miss.

# Hopscotch

Simple yet challenging—as many of the best games are—all you need is some chalk, permission to chalk out a grid, and a piece of wood or something similar for a puck. Hopscotch is one of the best-known and most enduring of children's games, as much loved today as it ever was. The game is played the world over, although the rules, and the grid, vary from country to country, even from district to district, but the basic principles remain the same—you throw your marker into numbered divisions and hop and jump your way from one end of the court to the other, and often back again, picking up your marker on the way, without transgressing any of the aforementioned rules. Easy! Actually, though, it isn't, and neither was it a hundred or so years ago. There were as many variations then as now, but on page 44 is one way to play!

PLAYING OUTSIDE

✳ Draw a grid on the ground, about 12 feet (3.5 meters) long, and choose your marker—a flat, sharp-edged pebble, flattened tin can, or bean bag.

✳ Draw a line a few steps from the grid, and from there toss your marker into square 1. It has to land inside the square without touching the border or bouncing out. If you don't get it within the lines, you lose your turn and pass the marker to the next person. If you do get it, however, go on to the next step.

✳ Miss out square 1 with your marker in it, and jump into squares 2 and 3, with both feet. You can't have more than one foot on the ground at a time, unless there are two numbered squares right next to each other (in this version, 2/3, 5/6, 8/9). In that case, you can put down both feet simultaneously (one in each square). Then hop and jump to the end of the grid. Always keep your feet inside the appropriate square(s); if you step on a line, hop on the wrong square, or step out of the square, you lose your turn.

✳ When you get to the last number, turn around (remaining on one foot) and hop and jump your way back in reverse order. While you're on the square right before the one with your marker, lean down and pick it up. Then, jump over that square and finish up.

✳ Pass the marker on to the next person. If you completed the course with your marker on square 1 (and without losing your turn), then throw your marker onto square 2 on your next turn. Your goal is to complete the course with the marker on each square. The first person to do this wins the game!

* Throwing your marker into the wrong division

* Stepping on a line

* Kicking it into the wrong division

* Touching the raised foot

* Landing your marker on a line

* Straddling when you should be hopping (putting two feet down in a single box)

## Origins

The story goes that Roman soldiers in Britain took part in a kind of hopscotch, wearing full armor and carrying heavy loads, using grids that were more than 100 feet (30 meters) long. Not much fun in that but this was no game; the purpose was to improve stamina. They must have looked quite a sight, so naturally children copied them, as children do, but presumably without the kit and on a much smaller scale. Somewhere along the line a scoring system was added and, over the years, the game in its various guises spread to every continent in the world.

The first recorded mention, in English anyway, comes in *The Book of Games* (an unfinished seventeenth century manuscript left by Francis Willughby and published in 2003 by Ashgate Publishing). The court seems to have been simpler then, either oblongs in a straight line from 1 to 6 or with the familiar one single, one double, one single and so on sets of squares up to 10 but including a couple of neutral zones.

*Webster's American Dictionary of the English Language* of 1828 included an entry for Scotch-hopper—"a play in which boys hop over scotches and lines in the ground." Scotch means a line drawn on the ground and Scotch-hopper was once the common name for hopscotch. In New York the game was very popular on the city streets, possibly brought by European immigrants, and was known as Potsies well into the twentieth century. The home base was the pot and the marker was the potsy. In Glasgow in Scotland, Peevers was the local name and the potsy, or peever, was a shoe-polish tin, empty of polish but filled with earth or stones.

# Marbles

Since mankind first walked the earth, people have been devising idle pastimes involving anything small, round, and rollable—pebbles, nuts, stones. Eventually, such was the interest, folk began to make small, round balls out of baked clay, then china, and by the mid 1800s, glass marbles were being made in Germany and Italy. But it wasn't until the early twentieth century that mass production came to the marble industry and hundreds of thousands of the little beauties rolled off the production line.

## Know the lingo

The youngsters of yesteryear knew the jargon and much of it has survived to the present day. Here are a few words it's still as well to know if you want your retro game to be authentic:

* **Mibs** Another name for marbles. Someone playing marbles is a mibster.

* **Taw** A specific marble, maybe slightly bigger than usual, used to roll or flick toward a target; also known as a shooter. A taw is also the line from behind which shots are taken.

* **Knuckle down** If a game is played "knuckle down," you must keep at least one knuckle on the ground while flicking your marble.

* **Roundings** This means moving along the taw to the best possible starting position, a tactic that can be thwarted by someone quick enough to shout, "Fen Roundings," in which case you have to stay where you are.

* **Keepsies** You get to keep the marbles you win; also called "in earnest" and "cut-throat."

* **For fair** You return all the marbles you've won to the original owners.

A whole host of games come under the banner heading of Marbles. They fall, and seemingly have always fallen, into two groups. Certainly they did in William Newell's day (*Games and Songs of American Children*, 1884). "One consists in striking the marbles out of a ring, by shooting from a line … the other, in making the tour of a series of holes made for the purpose." Below and on the next page are a few that were popular back in the day. Before you start, decide whether you're playing keepsies or for fair. The technique for shooting marbles is up to you, generally rolling or flicking, using the thumb.

## Conqueror

Make a line from where everyone is to roll their marbles. Someone starts by rolling a marble away randomly. The next player tries to hit it with his own marble and, if he does, collects both marbles, sending a new one out to start the game again. If he misses, the next player has a go and can aim for either marble. So it goes on. If a lucky, or skillful, player sends out a marble that sets up a chain reaction, so that several marbles are touched in that one turn, he gets to collect them all.

## Ring Taw

❉ Each player places the same number of marbles in the middle of a designated ring so as to make a circle.

❉ Order of play is decided by everyone rolling a marble from a distance away to see who can get closest to the ring.

❉ Whoever goes first tries to knock a marble out of the ring with his taw. If he fails, his turn is over. If he succeeds, he has another go from wherever the taw stopped and so on until he misses and the next in the order of play has a go.

❉ If the taw rolls out of the ring, that player's turn is over.

❉ If the taw is still in the ring at the end of a turn, it becomes a target and whoever hits it can claim a forfeit from the taw's owner (decide what it is to be beforehand).

❉ Whoever knocks most marbles out of the ring is the winner.

## Ringers

These days, Ring Taw is better known as Ringers. At the National Marbles Tournament (NMT), a competition for the under 14s held every June in New Jersey, the game is set up with 13 marbles arranged in a cross at the center of the ring, and if a taw is still in the ring at the end of the turn, it's just taken out, no forfeit required.

"Marrididdles are marbles made by oneself by rolling and baking common clay. By boys these are treated as spurious and are always rejected."

Alice Bertha Gomme, *The Traditional Games of England, Scotland and Ireland* (1894)

All marbles were given nicknames, depending on what they looked like. An aggie is one made from agate, an alley one made from alabaster, and an onionskin one that contains layered swirls of color. As a nickname, marrididdle seems a lot more imaginative than those, although it clearly didn't have much bartering value, since it was always rejected. Lady Gomme continues, "a bary = four stonies; a common white alley = three stonies. Those with pink veins being considered best. Alleys are the most valuable and are always reserved to be used as taws." We can probably guess what stonies were, but a bary?

# Nine Holes

Excavate nine small holes in the ground and mark a line a little way away from where to play. Players take turns in rolling their marbles down the holes, starting at one end and progressing in sequence to the other end. A miss means the turn is over. It's not clear why nine is significant and there seems to be no reason why this couldn't be five holes, or six or seven—maybe it's just that the more the holes, the harder it is.

If, instead of holes in the ground, a wooden board is used with arches cut in it, the game becomes Bridgeboard. Numbers are written over each archway and, traditionally, a marble through an archway means you win that number of marbles. If you miss, you lose your marble.

# CHASING GAMES

Doubtless children have chased one another in fun since time immemorial, and probably decided on some loose rules for their games, but not many authors or diarists thought to record them! Later authors were not so reticent. Joseph Strutt in his *Sports and Pastimes of the People of England* (1801) mentions Hunt the Fox (also known as Hunt the Hare)— a straightforward game in which one child is given a start and has to reach home base before the rest catch him. Many chasing games feature this idea of reaching a safe haven. Others revolve around one player, or group of players, preventing the other group from getting to a designated destination—in other words a wonderful excuse for all hell to break loose! Those of a delicate disposition or with an aversion to rough houses had better play something else since, even with the best of intentions, a little pushing and shoving and the odd robust response are inevitable.

# Tag

Someone is chosen to be "It", that is the one doing the chasing, usually by counting out (see page 24), and the others scatter while he tries to catch one of them. Once he has managed to touch someone, which is known as tagging, that person becomes It. Usually, a wall, bench, tree, or somewhere similar is nominated as a safe haven, where runners can go to catch their breath without fear of being tagged.

🖛 In Chain Tag, the person tagged takes It's hand and together they chase after the others. The next person tagged joins the last one and so a chain is formed. The first and last in the chain— the only ones with free hands—strive to tag those still on the run.

🖛 In Freeze Tag, the child tagged has to stay put, immobile, either in exactly the same position as when he was tagged or with arms stretched out to the side, until one of the others still on the loose manages to touch his hand or shoulder to release him. Once someone has been frozen three times, he becomes It. (In my young days, that game was called Releasio, a regular in recess (school break times) and a wonderful counterbalance to sitting at our desks, paying rapt attention to lessons!)

## Iron Tag

In *Games and Songs of American Children* (1884) William Newell suggests that the original game was Iron Tag, "once universal in the United States, and still here and there played." He cites an article about the game in the *Gentleman's Magazine* of February 1738, which notes that "the lad saves himself by the touching of cold iron," and "in later times this play has been altered amongst children of quality, by touching of gold instead of iron." Well, that one's no street game! The variations of Wood Tag and Stone Tag were undoubtedly much more common!

# British Bulldog

What a game! It has been banned from playgrounds and schoolyards for decades but that hasn't stopped kids from joyously having a go—and, providing some obvious ground rules are observed regarding allowable physical contact, it can be enormous fun for those of a more rumbustious nature. In this case, adult supervision is desirable, and possibly necessary, depending on who's playing!

One or two players, the bulldogs, start in the middle of the playing area and the others line up along one side. The bulldogs nominate one hapless child to run across to the opposite side with the intention of catching him as he does so. The very fleet of foot, and accomplished swervers, may elude the bulldogs (so, of course, they are not usually chosen); otherwise, once said child has been grabbed for long enough for a resounding yell of, "British bulldog, one, two, three," to ring out, he goes over to the catching crew. That's the signal for all the others to stampede across the playing area *en masse* while the bulldogs try to catch as many as possible. This sequence is repeated in the other direction and so it goes on until everyone is either a bulldog or exhausted. A simple-sounding game, but the potential for mayhem is clear—as more players become bulldogs, leaving fewer runners, the resemblance to a war zone becomes more marked!

## Barley-Brake

This game, well known in the Elizabethan age, sounds very like an early (and more genteel) version of the British Bulldog type of chasing game. According to William Newell in *Games and Songs of American Children* (1884) it is the forerunner of How Many Miles to Babylon?—and there's no reason why it shouldn't undergo a revival. The playing area is divided into three. A couple, boy and girl, stand in each of the outer areas, holding hands, and another boy and girl stand in the middle one, which is called "Hell." The middle pair, who must continue to hold hands and cannot leave their area, chase the others, who can separate if they like, as they attempt to change places. Once a boy is caught, he replaces the boy in the central couple, and likewise the girl. You can end the game when everyone's had a turn in "Hell" or just carry on until bedtime, as you like.

## Red Rover

In this variation the players line up opposite each other and link hands. One team says, "Red Rover, Red Rover, send Billy [or whomever it may be] right over." Billy then has to charge across, building up a head of speed, and keep going as fast as he can to try to break the link between two players in the opposite line (without breaking their wrists! In an outpouring of good sense, some players will let go hands without too much trouble, which may not be in the full spirit of the game, but if Billy is a big kid, who's quibbling?) If he succeeds, he takes one of the players he's run through back to join his team; otherwise, he joins the opposition. The game ends when all the players are on one side.

## How Many Miles to Babylon?

"Marlow, marlow, marlow bright,

How many miles to Babylon?"

"Threescore and ten."

"Can I get there by candlelight?"

"Yes, if your legs are as long as light,

But take care of the old gray witch by the roadside."

The players divide themselves into the familiar set-up—two groups on each side of the playing area, leaving one child in the middle. One group starts the above chant and, once it's done, the players dash toward each other intent on changing sides while the one in the middle catches as many as he can while trying to avoid being mown down. Once caught, the players turn into catchers. When everyone's a catcher, the game is over. In a version called Lil Lil, the even more unfortunate child in the middle has to touch a player three times on the back before he becomes a catcher.

# Capture the Flag

A tactical as well as a chasing game, Capture the Flag has been popular for many years. Two teams each have their own territory and their own flag, which need not be an actual flag but anything agreed upon—a coat, hat, towel, or an old T-shirt will do. The aim is to seize the other team's flag and return with it to your own territory while preventing your opponents from doing the same to you. The territories should be clearly defined, and the flag placed at the back to make it as difficult as possible for the opposition. To make it even harder, the flag is sometimes not placed in clear view and so has to be found first. This game is not as much of a total free-for-all as it may sound—there are rules:

- Players can be tagged in enemy territory only. In their own zone they are safe.

- If a player is tagged, there are several options. Teams should decided on which one is going to apply before the game starts. The options are, the tagged player:
  - is out of the game
  - joins the opposing team
  - is sent back to his own side (rather a tame option, this one!)
  - is sent to jail.

- The jail is a designated area at the back of the territory and as far away from the flag as possible.

- A player in jail may be freed by being tagged by one of his own side. He must return directly to his own territory (exempt from tagging) before launching any new attempt to reach the opposition's flag.

- The jailbreaker is free to carry on with his pursuit of the flag.

- If a player manages to grab the flag, he has to move fast, although he can hand it (not throw it) to one of his own side, if that's possible. If he's caught in possession, the flag is either returned to its original position or left where it is at the time of capture (decide beforehand). The carrier is sent to jail.

- The game ends when a player manages to carry the opposition's flag into his own home territory. Phew!

## Stealing Sticks

This is a similar game to Capture the Flag, often played by smaller children. Each side marks out a large goal at the rear of their half of the playing area, and a number of sticks (same for both sides) are laid separately along the goalline. The aim is for one side to steal all the other side's sticks, but the players must take just one at a time. Once in opposition territory on their way to the sticks, children may be tagged and sent to stand in the goal until freed by one of their own side. No one may steal a stick while a player is in the goal. If a child manages to elude his would-be captors and reach the goal untagged, on the way back, stick in hand, he is safe.

# Ringolevio

Many decades ago, the streets of New York and other big cities were filled with the youthful cries of boys and girls intent on capturing their opposite numbers and hauling them off to a special bench, porch, corner—wherever had been adopted as both home base and jail. This classic urban street game had become part of the culture, and it can certainly be adapted by today's kids, urban or not.

One team scatters within the predetermined field of play (which used to encompass several streets, backyards, rooftops, the bigger the better), the other counts to 50, or whatever is decided, and sets out in hot pursuit. When a child is caught, the catcher has to shout out a special chant and if the captive manages to wriggle free before it's finished, off he goes, still in the game. Otherwise captives must stay in jail until tagged free by one of their own side, not so easy as the jail is invariably guarded. Various chants were in vogue in different places—"Chain chain double chain, no break away," "Ringolevio, one-two-three, one-two-three, one-two-three." Moms and dads, grandmas, and granddads can put kids straight on their local chants. Once everyone, or nearly everyone, is in jail, the team's can swap roles and start again, unless it's already bedtime. In the old days, these games could go on for hours and hours!

## Relievo, or Bedlams

In Britain, a similar game to Ringolevio had already hit the streets. Jail was a chalked square referred to as the den and the guard was the "tenter," who had to have one foot in the den at all times, but just one—two or no feet meant any captives could escape; likewise if anyone else from the tenter's team put a foot in there. Once the opposition had scattered, they shouted, "Relievo," and the chasing team rushed after them, marching any captives back to the den. And "Relievo" was also the cry of the child who managed to dash triumphantly through the den without being caught by the tenter and so rescue his jailed teammates.

# Prisoner's Base

Apparently played in fourteenth century England, and mentioned by Shakespeare and Spenser in plays and poems, Prisoner's Base may well have been the inspiration for many other Tag-type games. As described by Joseph Strutt in *The Sports and Pastimes of the People of England* (1801), players form themselves into two equal groups and line up, holding hands in a chain, about 20 or 30 yards (18 or 27 meters) apart. Each group has a home base, with which the last one in the chain must always be in contact. One player peels off from his chain and is chased by someone from the opposition. Then another player runs out from the first chain and is similarly pursued and so on "until as many are out as choose to run, every one pursuing the man he first followed, and no other." If either of the pair succeeds in catching the other one, that's a point for the catcher's team. Both players return to their home chain and run out again as soon as the opportunity arises. The first team to reach a target score (decided in advance) wins. According to Strutt, "the number rarely exceeds twenty."

In other, possibly later, versions, captured players are taken to the catcher's home base and must stay there until freed by being tagged by one of their own side, which begins to sound rather like Ringolevio.

"... when the racing was over the men divided themselves into two parties and played prison base [otherwise known as prisoner's base, a boy's game in which each side tries to make prisoner the members of the opposing side who runs out of their base area], by way of exercise which we wish the men to take previously to entering the mountain ...

Captain Meriwether Lewis (1774–1809), the Lewis and Clark Expedition, part of Captain Lewis's journal entry for June 8, 1806

This sounds like an early version of Capture the Flag. The Corps of Discovery was encamped near a band of Nez Perce Indians, waiting for the snows to melt, and Captain Lewis, anxious about his men getting "lazy and slouthfull," encouraged them to play competitive games against the Indians, as well as dance to the violin!

# Hi Spy

Variously also known as Hy Spy, Hie Spy, and Ho Spy, this game has been played for centuries. Someone is chosen as the "Spy," home base selected, and everyone else runs to hide. A certain Mr Jamieson from Scotland takes up the story (in 1825): "The station which in England is called Home is here the Den, and those who keep it, or are the seekers, are called the Ins. Those who hide themselves, instead of crying 'Hoop' as in England, cry 'Hy Spy'; and they are denominated the Outs." All clear so far? "The business of the Ins is, after the signal is given, to lay hold of the Outs before they can reach the den. The captive then becomes one of the Ins; for the honor of the game consists in the privilege of hiding oneself." Nicely put! According to Joseph Strutt in *Sports and Pastimes of the People of England* (1801), the game is called Harry-racket or Hide and Seek (see page 88), and as well as captives becoming seekers, those who do the catching have "the privilege of hiding themselves."

In America, home base is also called the den, or hunk. Whoever is "It" closes his eyes, counts to a hundred (or 500 in fives) while everyone hides, and then off he goes to find them. Those in hiding have to reach home without being caught while It does his best to stop them. When It spots someone heading for home, he shouts, "I spy Jimmy," or whoever it is, and both kids make a dash for hunk. If It gets there first, he says, "One, two, three for Jimmy," and Jimmy is captured. If Jimmy gets there first, he says, "One, two, three for myself," and is free to hide again.

* In Yards Off, a stick is propped against hunk and someone throws it as far as he can. Whoever is It retrieves the stick and props it up again while everyone runs to hide. If anyone can reach hunk undetected, he throws down the stick and all captives are freed, so that It has to start again.

* In Kick the Can, a can or, these days, more likely a plastic bottle is placed somewhere in the playing area, separate from home base, or jail. Whoever is It runs to the can whenever he spies someone in order to call that person's name and send him to jail.
If the child who has been rumbled gets there first, though, and kicks the can, he is free to hide again. Anyone who kicks the can without having his name called frees all those in jail.

## Sheep and Wolf

Another very old game, in this one the roles are reversed. The wolf (It by any other name) does the hiding and the sheep (everyone else) cautiously try to find him. As soon as a sheep spots the wolf, he shouts, "I spy a wolf," and everyone makes a headlong dash for home with the wolf hot on their heels. Whoever falls into the wolf's clutches is the wolf next time around.

"O, the curly-headed varlets! —I must come to play at Blind Harry and Hy Spy with them."

Sir Walter Scott, *Guy Mannering* (1815)

# Duck on a Rock

The "duck" of the title is a stone, about the size of a fist, and the "rock" may actually be a rock, or it can be a post, stool, tree stump, anything with some height on which the duck may be positioned. Draw a line in the dirt, or chalk it on the ground, depending where you are, about 20 feet (6 meters) or so away from the rock. Then here's what you do:

✳ Everyone finds themselves a duck and, from behind the line, throws it at the rock. Whoever throws the nearest duck is the guard. In some older versions of the game, whoever is last to find a duck is the guard.

✳ The guard puts his duck on the rock and everyone takes turns in trying to knock it off by throwing their own duck at it from behind the line.

✳ In the case of a miss, the player has to retrieve his duck and get back over the line without being tagged by the guard (or he becomes the guard, and the guard becomes a thrower). If he makes it as far as his duck and puts his foot on it, however, the guard is not allowed to tag him, and he can stay there while others take their turn.

✳ If the duck is dislodged from the rock, the guard must replace it before he can tag anyone, so everyone trapped with their foot on their duck seizes the chance to rush back behind the line.

William Newell in *Games and Songs of American Children* (1884) ventures the opinion that "The game is not without a spice of danger from these missiles." Well, yes. The guard may find himself in a tricky situation, with everyone taking turns to throw stones in his vicinity. He may have to duck out of the way—perhaps that's where the name comes from! It may be a good idea to make a judicious substitution and for ducks to be beanbags or at least something softer than stones. If the substitute is too soft to knock the duck off the rock, maybe a rule adjustment to just touching it would be in order.

# Tom Tiddler's Ground

Draw a line on the ground. Whoever is going to be Tom Tiddler stands on one side, surrounded by much scattered gold and silver—or whatever you can find to represent such treasure, beanbags for example, small stones, cotton reels, old spoons, anything at all. Everyone else stands on the other side of the line and, when the game begins, they have to cross the line and gather up as much as they can, reciting, "Here we are on Tom Tiddler's ground, picking up gold and silver." Tom Tiddler has to try to catch the thieves, and any he does manage to grab are out. The last one caught is the new Tom Tiddler.

"And why Tom Tiddler's ground?" said the Traveller.

"Because he scatters halfpence to Tramps and such-like," returned the Landlord, "and of course they pick 'em up. And this being done on his own land (which it is his own land, you observe, and were his family's before him), why it is but regarding the halfpence as gold and silver, and turning the ownership of the property a bit round your finger, and there you have the name of the children's game complete."

Charles Dickens, *Tom Tiddler's Ground* (1861)

# BALL GAMES

Balls must be one of the earliest toys— a favorite of all age groups practically forever!— and archaeological finds seem to suggest that ball games are among the earliest of organized entertainments. Through the ages, all sorts of things have been used to make balls—animal bladders and skins, string and wool with a cloth covering, leather stuffed with wool, and, at least in Mesoamerica around 1600 BCE, solid rubber. Some real tennis balls (real tennis was the forerunner of lawn tennis) from the time of Henry VIII, discovered at Westminster Hall in London in the 1920s, were made from putty and human hair.

Children, as usual, improvised, and— anyway in Victorian times and doubtless earlier—rolled-up rags tied with string did very well for various throwing games. By the early twentieth century, though, the balls children played with were often made of hollow rubber and so had acquired a very satisfactory bounce. The appeal of the stick-and-ball games and bouncing-ball games devised by the kids of the day has never faded, and those games enjoyed by even earlier generations can still be played with modern rubber and tennis balls.

Boys and girls had been kicking around some form of ball for a thousand years and more before Charles Goodyear vulcanized rubber and invented the round ball in the mid nineteenth century. As vintage children's games go, soccer (football) has to be right up there at or near the top of the list. Kids just played with what they had—coats for goalposts, uneven teams, or no teams at all—everyone desperate for a touch of the ball. There may have been only one ball in the neighborhood and its owner would have been extremely popular after school when games started. A later generation felt the same. Eric Cantona, former international soccer player turned actor (born in 1966), mused, "I must admit that football in the streets gave us a great sense of freedom and liberty." Ah, the freedom of a kickabout. What could be better?

"Football united the kids. You didn't have to call for your mates; simply walking down the street bouncing a ball had the Pied Piper effect. We could all smell a game from 200 yards."

Sir Tom Finney (1922–2014),
legendary English soccer player

## Spaldeen

A small, pink, lightweight, rubber ball, beloved of street kids, especially in New York, the Spaldeen was a must-have for any number of street games. Spaldeen is thought to be derived from Spalding, the sporting goods company that produced their Hi-Bounce ball from the 1930s. The company stopped making it in the late 1970s but brought it back in 1999, using the name by which it was mostly known. Now Spaldeens are available in other colors, too, but pink is traditional.

# Ball against the Wall

Throwing a ball against a wall and catching it was always a pretty good start for a whole range of no-name ball games, played with a partner or solo. You can improvise all sorts of actions—catch with one hand and then the other; before catching, wait for the ball to bounce, clap hands four times, or behind your back, or turn around; bounce it under one leg; use two balls; and anything else you can think of. There are no real rules, other than those you decide upon yourself. What used to be the norm, though, was for ball players to recite various rhymes while performing these actions.

# Balls and Bonnets

This game was played in the days when children wore caps and hats. In the unsurprising event of not having enough of these to go round, try different colored plastic bowls or some other suitable receptacles. Each child must know which one is theirs. All the containers are lined up and, from a set distance away, the first child tries to throw a ball into any one of them. If he misses, a stone is placed in his bowl (any sort of counter will do but it was a stone in the old days) and he tries again. If he succeeds, everyone runs away except whoever has been allocated the bowl the ball lands in. That player's task is to collect the ball as quickly as he can and then shout, "Stop!" Once everyone has come to a shuddering halt, he has to throw the ball (gently!) at one of them. If he scores a hit, that player has a stone put in his bowl. If the thrower misses, he gets the stone. The first player to collect six stones loses. Count up everyone's stones and the one with the fewest wins.

## 1, 2, 3, O'Leary

If no wall is available, try this old favorite. Bounce the ball on the ground on the numbers, pass your leg over the ball on "O'Leary," backward or forward, and then catch it when the rhyme indicates. Any size ball will do.

1, 2, 3, O'Leary

4, 5, 6, O'Leary

7, 8, 9, O'Leary

10 O'Leary, caught it!

## Ball against the Wall rhyme

"Nebuchadnezzar, King of the Jews
Bought his wife a pair of shoes
When the shoes began to wear
Nebuchadnezzar began to swear
When the swearing had to stop
Nebuchadnezzar bought a shop
When the shop began to sell
Nebuchadnezzar bought a bell
When the bell began to ring
Nebuchadnezzar began to sing:"

Then comes a nursery rhyme, often "Humpty Dumpty." However, if you happen to drop the ball along the way, you have to start again from the beginning, so getting as far as the nursery rhyme is not a foregone conclusion.

# Keep Away/Piggy in the Middle

There are three players; two throw the ball to each other while the third one, standing between them, tries to intercept it—an old game that never loses its capacity to entertain. If more than three want to play, everyone stands in a circle and players have to lob the ball across the ring while the one in the middle is led a merry dance, jumping and running and dodging, attempting to capture it. Once she does, she swaps places with either the bad thrower or the bad catcher. Decide who it is to be in advance to avoid squabbles. If the one in the middle is much shorter than most of the others, allowing the ball to bounce once is a kindness.

## Keep Ball

This old game has no special name, but the whole idea is to keep the ball ... Instead of a single person in the middle, it's a whole team! Members of one side pass the ball among themselves while players in the other team try to intercept. That's it—straightforward but fun! Whichever team has the ball at the end of the game wins.

# Ante Over

You need a gabled building (not too high) or some structure that has a sloping roof (both sides) to play this game nineteenth century style. However, as with all children's games, improvisation is the key and any barrier that divides the two teams so that they can't see each other will do.

Someone throws the ball over the roof randomly and if anyone from the waiting side manages to catch it, he dashes around to the other side of the building and attempts to hit one of the opposition with the ball. As soon as he appears, the opposition scatter, of course, and the ball-carrier can either throw the ball quickly or chase someone until he's close enough not to miss. Anyone so struck goes over to the opposition, and so it goes on until all the players are on one side. According to William Newell in *Games and Songs of American Children* (1884), the excitement of the game lies in having to be prepared "to see an adversary suddenly appear, ball in hand, and ready to throw." Anticipation is all!

In later versions, there appear to be a few more rules:

- The players from whose side the ball is initially flung have to shout, "Ante over," so the others know it's on its way, and if no one catches it, play switches and that side shout the same while lobbing it back.

- If the ball doesn't make it over the roof but falls back, the thrower shouts, "Pigtails," (goodness knows why!) to appraise the other side of the situation, and then has another try.

- Once the catcher appears, the opposition take to their heels and run around the building, ball-carrier in hot pursuit. Anyone who makes it back to their own side without being hit is safe, at least until the next time.

THE SATURDAY EVENING POST

An ... kly ... Franklin
Founded ...

5c. the Copy
7c. in Canada
INCLUDING TAX

August 10, 1940

VOLUME 213  NUMBER 6

"All of this has happened before, and it will all happen again."

J.M. Barrie, *Peter Pan* (1904)

# Stickball

A rudimentary form of baseball or rounders, this game was hugely popular on twentieth century American urban streets right up until the late 1970s. All that was needed was a broom handle and either a rubber ball or a tennis ball, and maybe some chalk with which to draw a strike zone on a backstop—usually a convenient wall. Manhole covers were often the bases and other features chosen for boundary lines. You can still play the old-fashioned game; indeed, these days there are organized Stickball leagues. The rules haven't changed much, even if the location has—the backyard, disused parking lot, park, or some similar open space are all infinitely preferable to a street full of cars.

For the fast-pitch game you need to chalk a rectangle on the wall for the strike zone, and you can play with just two or three players, or even one, per team. If the batter swings and misses, or doesn't swing, and the ball has chalk on it, that's counted as a strike; if it doesn't have chalk on it, that's a ball. (As in baseball, three strikes and the batter's out; four balls and the batter moves to first base.) In the slow-pitch game, you don't need the wall, just someone to play backstop. The pitcher lobs the ball sidearm from about 40 feet (12 meters) or so away and the batter thwacks it after one bounce. In either version, you run around bases if there's enough space for these to have been designated, or devise a way to score depending on where the ball lands or hits surrounding buildings.

## Fungo

This is a way of playing Stickball by yourself. You toss the ball in the air, let it bounce once, and then slog it as hard as you can. Some people let it bounce twice or not at all. The choice is yours but, as with all forms of the game, you need plenty of space and no nearby windows! Of course, if you are playing on your own, you have to retrieve the ball yourself. All good exercise! Some organized Stickball leagues specialize in this form of the game.

Chapter 3

PARTY TIME

The idea of a party sends a thrill through most children, especially if it's being held in their honor, but even if the gathering is of mixed age groups, such as at Christmas or for a family occasion, it can be just as exciting for young ones. Whatever the event may be, keeping the children entertained has got to be high on the list of priorities, and games play a major part in that.

So what makes a good children's party game? First and foremost, everyone has to be involved for all or most of the time. No one should feel left out, so any turns have to be kept short. Kids can be encouraged to Pin the Tail on the Donkey quite quickly, for instance, and the tail ending up on its nose or in its ear is partly the point of the game.

Children can't be expected to be on their best behavior all the time, though, especially when excited. All that exuberance needs an outlet. A few more boisterous games will use up some energy and keep everyone happy, even if they do tire out a few, which may not be a bad thing. Organize games to be played outside if the weather's good, and keep them traditional.

"Anything is good if it's made of chocolate."

Jo Brand, comedian, writer, and actor

# RINGS AND ARCHES

Little children holding hands and dancing around in a circle is a timeless activity. Ring and arch games no doubt developed from this, and they are as diverse as can be imagined, older children adding to the mix with their own inventions.

## Hunt the Slipper

This is almost the same as the well-known game of Pass the Slipper. Here's how it was played in 1916 (*My Book of Indoor Games*, Clarence Squareman). All the children except one sit in a ring. They are the cobblers and the one left outside is the customer. The customer leaves a shoe, or slipper, with the cobblers to be mended, saying, "Cobbler, cobbler, mend my shoe. Get it done by half-past two." The cobblers pass the slipper around as quickly as they can, hiding it as much as possible, while the customer stands back and is supposed not to look. After a minute, the customer comes back to the circle and demands his shoe, but the cobblers tell him it's not ready. So the customer tries to decide who's got it, inspecting everyone closely. The cobblers continue to pass the shoe around surreptitiously, behind his back, while contriving to look as innocent as possible. Who, me? Once the customer finds his shoe, whoever is in possession becomes the new customer.

# Pass the Parcel

This requires some pre-party organizing. The parcel is created on the Russian doll principle—a parcel within a parcel within a parcel, as many parcels as you can manage, and all tied so as to be difficult to undo. (Better to do it yourself than to buy a kit.) The item thus elaborately wrapped can be anything you choose, such as a small toy or some candy. While the music plays, the children pass the parcel around the circle. When the music stops, the child in possession starts to undo it—that is, tear at the paper to get it off as quickly as possible. When the music starts again, the parcel must be passed on, just as it is, paper hanging off or not. Gradually, the parcel gets smaller and smaller, and the tearing more frenzied, until, eventually, one lucky child manages to wrench off the last of the wrapping before the music starts again and triumphantly claims the prize.

"Only where children gather is there any real chance of fun."

Mignon McLaughlin,
journalist and author

# Hunt the Squirrel

All the children sit in a circle, except one who walks around the outside of it, holding a knotted handkerchief and reciting the following:

"Hunt the squirrel through the wood,

I lost him, I found him;

I have a little dog at home,

He won't bite you,

He won't bite you,

And he will bite you."

She can pass by as many children as she likes saying "He won't bite you," but when she gets to "And he will bite you," she touches whoever she is standing behind with the knotted handkerchief, drops it, and takes to her heels around the circle. The child so identified grabs the hanky and dashes off in the opposite direction. When they meet, they have to curtsy three times before continuing the headlong rush. Whoever gets to the vacant space first claims it; the slower one becomes the new hunter.

## Variations on a theme

Many variations of Hunt the Squirrel existed in the old days, all with different verses to recite. The principle of the games is the same, though, and for each one you can use those verses given here, make up some of your own words to do the job of selecting the chaser, or not have a verse at all.

### Drop the Handkerchief

Much the same as Hunt the Squirrel except the children stand and join hands, and the circler is chased around the outside of the ring by his opponent until he is caught and tagged with the handkerchief. In another version, the handkerchief is dropped quietly, no reciting or shoulder tapping, so the circler has a head start in racing around the circle before his opponent even realizes she's supposed to be doing the chasing.

## Cat after Mouse, or Threading the Needle

The child selected to be the mouse taps one of the circle, who gives chase. The mouse can dive under linked hands to run in and out of the circle at will. The cat, in hot pursuit, must follow the mouse's route exactly. In some versions, those in the circle raise their arms to let the mouse through and lower them to obstruct the cat. Once caught, the cat takes the mouse's place, and the mouse becomes the cat.

## Duck, Duck, Goose

The circler, sometimes referred to as the fox, touches each player sitting in the ring, saying, "Duck … duck," until she decides to call one a goose. The goose scrambles up and, in something of a reversal of roles, chases the fox around the ring, trying to catch her before she can get to the vacant space. Whoever loses that race is the next fox.

## I Wrote a Letter to My Love

The difference with this game is that the children dance in a circle, reciting the verse below, and the circler moves around them in the opposite direction. When they get to "pocket," the circler taps the nearest child and the chase commences.

"A-tisket a-tasket
A green and yellow basket
I wrote a letter to my love
And on the way I dropped it,
I dropped it,
I dropped it,
And on the way I dropped it.
A little boy he picked it up
and put it in his pocket."

"Somehow this amused them almost all the long spring afternoon. Different children took turns holding the May poles and sometimes they would even form a procession and hippity-hop around the park. They paraded down Main Street for a little way, but came back to the park in time to play 'Drop the Handkerchief,' 'Hide and Seek,' and 'Tag,' before refreshments were served."

Emily Rose Burt, *Entertaining Made Easy* (1919)

Ms Burt's May pole Party for Children featured cleverly improvised May poles that clearly delighted this party of girls and boys, but didn't deter them from playing a few other traditional games as well.

# Change Seats

A wonderful scrum of a game, this was, apparently, popular in the Victorian era. Players seat themselves in a circle, on chairs, and someone stands in the middle repeating, "Change seats, change seats," but no one moves until he adds, "The king's come." Then everyone tries to follow the instruction, caller included.

"The sport lies in the bustle in consequence of every one's endeavoring to avoid the misfortune of being the unhappy individual who is left without a seat," says Alice Bertha Gomme in *The Traditional Games of England, Scotland and Ireland* (1894). "The principal actor often slily says, 'The king's not come,' when, of course, the company ought to keep their seats; but from their anxious expectation of the usual summons, they generally start up, which affords a great deal of merriment." Well, you can see that it would!

The person in the middle asks the question of someone seated in the circle. If the answer is no, the people on either side of the speaker have to swap seats, before the questioner can slip in instead. Alternatively, the answer may be a qualified yes—"Yes, except people wearing blue," or "Yes, except people with fair hair," in which case all those wearing blue or with fair hair have to swap places as quickly as possible, and the questioner has a better chance of grabbing one. Whoever's left standing is the next questioner.

# The Feather

Children sit closely together in a circle, someone drops a big feather among them, and they have to blow it up and away. If it lands on them, they pay a forfeit (see page 28). I remember playing a similar game with balloons at Christmas time, as many as we had all at the same time. We weren't sitting in a circle, just around the room, children and adults alike, and the idea was simply not to let any balloon touch the floor—or fall on the fire, or pop on the Christmas tree. It was pandemonium, and enormous fun!

# Earth, Air, Fire, and Water

You need a soft ball, beanbag, or knotted handkerchief for this. Once the children have sat down in a circle, one of them throws the ball to another child, citing one of the elements. The child who catches it has to name something that lives in that element before a count of ten, unless "Fire" is called. Then she must keep quiet before throwing the ball to someone else. Any transgression means a forfeit (see page 28). The game can go on for as long as you like, and to keep everyone's interest, you could change the categories to Bird, Beast, or Fish. None of these necessitates silence, and you mustn't repeat any creature that has been named before.

"It is almost impossible to imagine the excitement that is produced by this game when it is played with spirit, and the fun is not altogether confined to the players, as it gives almost as much enjoyment to those who are looking on."

Clarence Squareman, *My Book of Indoor Games* (1916)

Mr Squareman obviously had a good time watching children of his acquaintance playing The Feather. Perhaps he should've joined in!

# Oranges and Lemons

A hundred or so years ago, no self-respecting hostess would deny young party-goers a few rounds of this game. Two children join hands to form an arch, deciding between them which one is oranges and which one lemons. The others line up and skip under the arch, turning around one way to join the back of the line, skipping under again, and then going around the other way, and so on. All the while everyone sings the rhyme (see opposite), which is based on the bells of old London churches. When it comes to the last line of the song, the arch children lower their arms slowly as the others continue to run under, faster now, and at the very last word the arch drops down and captures a child *in situ*. She has to whisper her choice of fruit to her captors and line up behind the appropriate side of the arch. When everyone has been caught and lined up on one side or the other, they finish with a Tug o' War.

# London Bridge is Falling Down

Nothing is certain about the origins of this game except they go way back. Whether the song or the game came first is not known and all anybody seems to agree on is that it probably refers to an actual incident, but exactly what and when is open to conjecture. The old London Bridge certainly crumbled a bit, and underwent extensive alterations and repairs. A new one replaced it in 1831 and this is the one that was deconstructed and then reconstructed, brick by brick, in Lake Havasu City, Arizona, in the 1970s.

The game is played like Oranges and Lemons but the children in line hold on to the waist or shoulders of the one in front as they pass under the arch. In England, the children dance around in a circle first, before two of them form the arch, and they dispense with the Tug o' War.

"Oranges and lemons,

Say the bells of St Clement's;

You owe me five farthings,

Say the bells of St Martin's;

When will you pay me,

Say the bells of Old Bailey;

When I grow rich,

Say the bells of Shoreditch;

When will that be?

Say the bells of Stepney;

I'm sure I don't know,

Says the Great Bell of Bow.

Here comes a light to light you to bed;

Here comes a chopper to chop off your head;

The last, last, last, last man's head."

The old rhyme as given by Alice Bertha Gomme in *The Traditional Games of England, Scotland and Ireland* (1894). Latterly, the last line is more frequently: "Chip, chop, chip chop, last man's dead."

London Bridge is falling down

Falling down, falling down

London Bridge is falling down

My fair lady

This is just the first verse of many, and by no means the only version.

The oldest seems to be:

London Bridge is broken down,

Dance o'er my lady lee,

London Bridge is broken down,

With a gay lady.

All the verses go on to describe how to build up the bridge again and then watch over it.

# Ring a Ring o' Roses

In this simple game for younger children, those playing link hands and skip or walk around in a circle, singing the rhyme. On the last line they follow instructions and all fall down, causing much laughter. The game is based around an old, old rhyme with many variations and origins lost in history. A popular interpretation used to be that it refers to the great plague pandemics that swept Europe in the fourteenth century, or the one that most famously ravaged London in 1665, but this theory has fallen out of favor. Truth is no one knows for certain what it's about.

Ring a Ring o' Roses
A pocket full of posies
Atishoo! Atishoo!
All fall down.

PARTY TIME

## Ring around the Rosie

In Britain, all the rhymes include sneezing, but not so in America. William Newell in *Games and Songs of American Children* (1884) calls it Ring around the Rosie and suggests several versions that were once in vogue in various cities. In one a child stands in the center of the ring, apparently representing a rose tree, and the last one down at the end changes places with her. The song is:

> Round the ring of roses,
>
> Pots full of posies,
>
> The one who stoops last
>
> Shall tell whom she loves best.

Not much going for that one in the rhyming stakes!

# SNEAKING UP AND "DO AS I DO"

Who of a certain age has not played these games at a birthday party or at school in their younger days? They may well be twentieth century versions of games that have been played for hundreds of years, but these are the ones we know and love.

## What Time is it, Mr Fox?/ What's the Time, Mr Wolf?

Whoever is chosen to be Mr Fox (or Mr Wolf, depending on which side of the Atlantic you happen to be) stands a distance away from the other players and with his back to them. The others stand along an imaginary line (or a real one, if you like) facing him. When everyone's ready, the children chorus, "What time is it, Mr Fox?" and Mr Fox answers with a number o'clock—three o'clock, four o'clock, whatever he likes, while turning to face them. The children take that number of steps forward, Mr Fox turns away, and the crowd asks again. So it goes on until Mr Fox decides it's "Dinner time!" and chases the step-takers back to the start line. If he catches one for dinner, that's the new Mr Fox.

1

2

3

## Red Light, Green Light

The world's first electric traffic lights were installed in America in the early part of the the twentieth century, so it's unlikely this game is older than that! The set-up is the same as for What Time is it, Mr Fox? Whoever is standing out front, back to the crowd, shouts, "Green light," as the signal for everyone to move. Then he shouts, "Red light," as he turns to face the players, who must stop instantly. Anyone he spots moving so much as a muscle has to go back to the start. First to reach him is the new traffic controller.

## Statues/Grandmother's Footsteps

There's no shouting in this variation. When everyone's ready, Grandma turns her back and everyone else rushes toward her. The first to tag her takes a turn out front. The drawback is that she can turn around at any time and everyone has to freeze—and it's hard to do that instantly if you're running fast. Any movement, including involuntary giggles, means back to the start, and she can take a walk around the "statues" to check. That may be an opportunity for a fearless few to sneak forward quietly—although, being Grandma, she may have eyes in the back of her head!

# Mother May I?

This starts out similar to the Mr Fox game (see page 84), but Mother faces the line of children. In some versions, she asks each child to perform a task, in others the children take turns to request permission. In either case, the dialogue continues along the same lines. So she may say, "Sam, take two giant steps forward," to which Sam must respond, "Mother, may I take two giant steps forward?" Mother has the option to confirm or deny permission, or she may say, "No, you may not, but you may froghop forward three times," or, "run backward for two seconds," or anything similar that takes her fancy. Woe betide the child who forgets to ask, "Mother may I?" It's back to the start for her, and likewise anyone who tries to creep forward while Mother's attention is directed elsewhere. The aim is to be the first to reach Mother and so take over that commanding role.

## Simon Says

Stand up, sit down, hop on one leg, pull a funny face—anything Simon tells you to do, you must do, or at least attempt to do, but only if preceded by the words, "Simon says ..." Otherwise out you go. Simon may issue instructions quite fast, so you have to concentrate to keep up and not automatically follow orders without hearing, "Simon says," first. Last one in is the next Simon. If "Simon says stand on your head," several players may elect to drop out at once!

> "Happiness is not something ready made. It comes from your own actions."
>
> Dalai Lama (b. 1935), Buddhist leader and winner of the Nobel Peace Prize

# Follow My Leader

A line of children follows the chosen leader around the room, doing whatever he's doing—jogging, skipping, marching, turning around, hands on head or hips or clasped behind, waving arms in the air—until time's up and another leader takes over. To get to that point, the leader can take his followers around in ever-decreasing circles into the center of the room so the children are wound up tightly, and then instruct them to turn around and run back the way they came to unwind the spiral. Hence another old name for the game, Running Maze.

That's how it was in 1916 according to Clarence Squareman (*My Book of Indoor Games*). However, back in the day, Follow My Leader was much more of a romp. According to Alice Bertha Gomme in *The Traditional Games of England, Scotland and Ireland* (1894), this was an outdoor game and the leader strode off across fields, through woods, up trees, down trees, over gates, across streams, and back again, the line of followers doing exactly the same. What fun that would be, but not necessarily convenient for a party since it probably took a very long time! What you could do is construct a suitable obstacle course in the yard, or hall, or big living room, moving anything fragile, or precious, out of the way, and let the kids get on with it. Be prepared for shrieks, a few tumbles, and a lot of happy, if disheveled party guests!

Searching games are always fun. It may be a good idea to define the play area, especially for Hide and Seek indoors, if you don't want a horde of inquisitive children swarming all over the house.

## Hide and Seek

Some version of this classic children's game has probably been played since the dawn of time—kids hide and someone looks for them. At its most straightforward, that's how it's played still. One child is chosen to be "It". She covers her eyes and counts to ten or twenty, or whatever's been decided, while everyone else scatters and finds a niche in which to wait to be found. The seeker shouts when she's finished counting, or just quietly sets out on the hunt. Whoever is found first is the next It and whoever is found last is the winner of the round. In some versions, instead of waiting to be found, those in hiding can sneak back to the start (see Hi Spy, page 58), and the seeker can call an amnesty by shouting, "Olly, olly, oxen free," (reason unknown!), when everyone comes back to the start to begin again, or the party games move on to something else.

### Names aplenty

"Apodidraskinda, the game of hide and seek, played by the children in Greece, exactly as in our days. It is represented in a painting found at Herculaneum."

William Smith, William Wayte, G.E. Marindin, *A Dictionary of Greek and Roman Antiquities* (1890)

Greek grammarian and teacher Julius Pollux described Apodidraskinda in the second century, and sixteenth-century lexicographer Richard Huloet apparently mentioned King By Your Leave in his English–Latin dictionary—both Hide and Seek by any other name. The same could be said for Hi Spy and all its variations (see page 58).

## Sardines

The same principle as Hide and Seek but with a twist (sometimes literally!). One person hides and all the others go looking for her. When a seeker pulls back the right curtain or excavates the right bush, instead of shouting with glee, she squeezes into the same hiding place and they wait together, quiet as mice. When someone else finds them, she does the same thing and so on. As the hiding place becomes more and more cramped, and the seekers-cum-hiders more and more contorted, giggles become impossible to stifle and so the hiding place is more and more obvious. The last one to find them loses.

"One of life's primal situations; the game of hide and seek. Oh, the delicious thrill of hiding while the others come looking for you, the delicious terror of being discovered, but what panic when, after a long search, the others abandon you! You mustn't hide too well. You mustn't be too good at the game. The player must never be bigger than the game itself."

Jean Baudrillard (1929–2007), sociologist and philosopher

In my experience, not being found is never a problem!

# Lookabout

This is the Victorian version of Hunt the Thimble, or Thimble in Sight as William Newell calls it in *Games and Songs of American Children* (1884). Choose a small item to be hidden—could be a thimble or a button or a pen. Everyone leaves the room except the person doing the hiding. She places the item discreetly, so it's visible but easily overlooked—not in a drawer or under the carpet, for example; it should be possible to see it without anything being moved. Then the others come back in and try to find it. The rule is when you spot it, you sit down without saying anything. The tactic is first to move away and glance elsewhere, to fool anyone who may be watching you. Last person standing hides the item next time.

You can play this outside, too, maybe with a slightly larger item, such as a ball, and for younger children it may be better to have a larger item in any case.

## Hot Boiled Beans and Bacon

In this variation of Lookabout, described by Clarence Squareman in *My Book of Indoor Games* (1916), one child is the seeker and everyone else does the hiding. Once the item's hidden, the seeker is summoned back into the room by everyone calling out together, "Hot Boiled Beans and Bacon; it's hidden and can be taken." As the seeker looks around, the others give her clues by saying she's "cold" or "very cold" (nowhere near), "hot" or "very hot" (getting much closer), or "burning" (almost touching it); or, according to William Newell, "the search is directed by magical music, which grows louder as the person comes nearer to his object." Magical music—what a lovely idea!

I played this as a child but it was called How Green You Are, and the clues were given by saying that phrase loudly or softly, depending on how close the seeker strayed to the hidden treasure—loud meant close, very loud meant very close and it could get very loud indeed! This was also a technique for I Spy with My Little Eye (see page 106) if the guessers were having trouble locating the answer.

# GAMES YOU CAN'T IGNORE

These old games are the fallback situation. If no one can decide what they want to play, or everyone wants to play something different, suggesting one of these may restore harmony.

## Blind Man's Buff

In one form or another, this game has been played, by children and adults alike, for well over a thousand years. No need to go back that far for a retro version! Try it as it was played in 1916, according to Clarence Squareman in *My Book of Indoor Games*. He also describes a similar game, Blind Man's Wand (see opposite).

Clear the room, or yard space, of obstacles and blindfold whoever is to be the blind man. Then comes a set question and answer routine.
"How many horses has your father got?" the party-going crowd must ask.
"Three."
"What color are they?"
"Black, white, and gray."
"Turn round three times and catch whom you may," everyone shouts as they scatter.

The blindfolded one is turned around three times to disorientate her. Then, arms automatically outstretched, she has to stumble around in search of a fellow party-goer, all of whom are lurking in the vicinity, making little noises to attract her, and then moving swiftly away, probably giggling. Once she finally manages to grab someone, she has to guess who it is and, if she's right, that child is the next one to be blindfolded.

Two hundred-plus years ago, the game was a tad rougher. Joseph Strutt in *The Sports and Pastimes of the People of England* (1801) describes the blindfolded player as being "buffeted by his comrades until he can catch one of them." ("Buff" is an old word for "a blow.") This was how the game was played in ancient Greece, where they used knotted cloth to beat the blindfolded one. Up until the middle of the eighteenth century or so, the game was called Hoodman Blind because players were blindfolded by turning their headgear around, hoods being the natty headwear of the day.

> "But now for Blind man's Buff they call;
>
> Of each encumbrance clear the hall—
>
> Jenny her silken 'kerchief folds,
>
> And blear-eyed Will the black lot holds."
>
> William Blake, *Poetical Sketches* (1783)

## Blind Man's Wand

No possibility of buffeting in this version of Blind Man's Buff. The blindfolded player stands in the middle of the others, holding a wand, which can be a long twig or made of rolled-up paper. To be truly retro, "someone then plays a merry tune on the piano, and the players dance round and round the blind man, until suddenly the music stops." Okay, improvise! Then everyone stands still, the blind man reaches out with the wand, and whomever it touches has to take hold of it and imitate any sound the blind man chooses to make—the barking of a dog, for instance, the clucking of a hen. The idea is for the blindfolded one to identify the person on the other end of the wand by the voice. If he gets it right, they swap places. If not, he keeps the blindfold for another round. That must concentrate the mind somewhat!

# Musical Chairs

Line up the chairs, one fewer than the number of people playing, in the most convenient way for the space you have—in a circle, in a line alternating the way the chairs face, in two lines back to back. Someone not playing should be in charge of the music. Everyone strolls by the chairs, keeping close because when the music stops, that's the signal to sit down on the nearest one. Fast reactions are required and the child left standing is out. Remove a chair and play the music again. Carry on until two children and just one chair are left. Only one winner!

❧ In Musical Bumps you dispense with the chairs and, when the music stops, the children sit on the ground. Last one down is out.

❧ In Musical Statues, the children must remain in exactly the same position they are in when the music stops. Anyone who moves is out.

PARTY TIME

## The Sea King

In this fishy version of Musical Chairs, the children sit in a circle, each one choosing the name of a fish. Whoever is chosen to be the sea king starts off in the middle and then runs around the ring calling out the fishy names, in any order. As their names are called, the children get up and follow him. When everyone is milling about, he suddenly says, "The sea is troubled," and sits down, swiftly followed by all the fishes. Last one down is the new king.

# Reverend Crawley's Game

If the Reverend Crawley, whoever he may have been, really did invent this game, one thing's for sure. He was a man with a sense of humor. Challenging for gymnastic types and any would-be yogis, this forerunner of Twister seems to be never less than a hoot!

You need at least seven or eight players, but the more the merrier. Everyone stands in a circle and holds hands but not with the person next door and not both with the same person. The result is an enormous tangle and, once that's achieved (not easy in itself!), the task is to untangle it without letting go of hands. Oh what a mass of wriggling and twisting and crawling ensues! What gap to climb through? What arm to limbo under? The kids have to work it out together and, eventually, after much giggling and healthy exercise, they end up back in a circle, or sometimes two— allegedly! This is not a game I've tried so I've no idea how many times the tangle collapses in a mangled heap of shrieking kids! Actually, I feel rather deprived.

# Calm down

Two games to counteract all the excitement:

## Sleeping Lions

This twentieth century, end-of-party game is still popular because it is effective in quietening everyone down after a lot of romping around. The children lie down and pretend to be asleep (it doesn't matter if they are lions, tigers, fairies, pixies, or anything else). One or two others (could be older children) move among them and gently try to make them laugh. Decide beforehand if tickling is to be allowed. Anyone who succumbs is out, so the winner is the last one sleeping despite the enormous temptation to giggle.

## Judge and Jury

In this sitting-down game from 1916 (*My Book of Indoor Games*, Clarence Squareman) the children sit in two rows, facing each other, and one is chosen to be Judge. She asks one of the other players a question (which can be anything) and here's the catch. Whomever she asks must not say a word. The person sitting opposite must reply. One word answers don't count, it must be two or more, and "Yes," "No," "Black," "White," and "Gray" are forbidden. Any mistake leads to a forfeit (see page 28).

"One of the luckiest things that can happen to you in life is, I think, to have a happy childhood."

Agatha Christie (1890–1976), the world's best-selling novelist

Chapter 4

# PARLOR

# GAMES

A charming, old-fashioned word for a charming, old-fashioned concept—the parlor was the room that was kept for best, somewhere to receive visitors, where only the best china was used. In plenty of households, though, it was also a place for relaxation, entertainment, and hobbies, where the family gathered in the afternoons and evenings to read, sew, play games—no sophisticated electronic devices then to distract and absorb young minds (or old ones, come to that), not even television.

Parlor games tended to be sedate rather than boisterous—Charades is probably the most active, although if children's parties made it to the parlor, that idea was likely to have been turned on its head, and any precious, breakable items judiciously removed before the Blind Man's Buff started. I've included games of the more rambunctious variety in the chapter on party games (see page 70), even though some of them undoubtedly found their way into the parlor, especially the musical ones, because that's where the piano resided.

"There is nothing so contagious as the spirit of play."

Clarence Squareman, *My Book of Indoor Games* (1916)

Aside from special occasions, guessing and word games, cards, and board games were normal activities, played often, and by whoever was available. They were fun for all the family to join in—and maybe kids discovered that you don't have to expend a lot of physical energy to let your creativity and imagination run wild.

# GUESSING GAMES

Children's games that depend on exercising the brain have to be absorbing and entertaining or the participants will lose interest and take to running around again, or at least going off to do something else. Here are a few that did the trick in the old days.

My first makes all nature appear of one face;

At the next we find music, and beauty and grace;

And, if this Charade is most easily read,

I think that the third should be thrown at my head.

Answer: snowball
A typical poetic charade from over two hundred years ago.

I talk, but I do not speak my mind

I hear words, but I do not listen to thoughts

When I wake, all see me

When I sleep, all hear me

Many heads are on my shoulders

Many hands are at my feet

The strongest steel cannot break my visage

But the softest whisper can destroy me

The quietest whimper can be heard.

Answer: an actor. The poetic charade survived into the twentieth century. This one is said to have been one of Theodore Roosevelt's (1858–1919) favorites.

## Charades

Hands up who has never played Charades! Not many takers for that one, I daresay, but who knew that its origins lie in the riddles and proverbs of Renaissance Europe, and that it started off as a game for adults? Rumor has it that Louis XIV of France and Catherine the Great of Russia were both aficionados—apparently, Louis once danced the clues to the assembled company!

At first, speaking was allowed, in rhyme or prose, and although this idea of poetic Charades has survived, another silent version soon became just as popular. Clues were given in exaggerated mime with strictly no moving the lips! After a while this "dumb Charade" evolved into the more elaborate and challenging "acting Charade." Not just single words, although that was still common, but well-known phrases, plays, places —anything that all the players decided was okay, really—were enacted for the delectation of fellow party-goers.

This was the game that took the drawing rooms of eighteenth- and nineteenth-century society by storm —one team acted out each syllable of their chosen word and then the whole word for the other team to guess. Not competitive, speed immaterial, playing Charades became a fashionable evening entertainment, although children were allowed to join in, and undoubtedly played their own version among themselves.

Examples from literature describe the participants throwing themselves into the acting in a big way, improvising costumes and props—Mr Rochester, his ward little Adele, and house guests under Jane's somewhat sardonic eye in Charlotte Bronte's *Jane Eyre* (1847); Becky Sharp impressing the king and everyone else in William Thackeray's *Vanity Fair* (1848).

## Children's favorite

By the turn of the twentieth century, the game of Charades had become a staple of children's parties at every level of society, and it was played enthusiastically when and wherever families and friends got together for celebrations of all sorts. In America in the 1930s, 1940s, and later, a more competitive version, referred to as "The Game," was all the rage. Players were divided into two teams, as usual. Each team nominated someone in the opposing team to do the acting and gave them the chosen word, phrase, or name. The players then had a set time to guess what it was from their fellow team-member's mime. The teams vied with each other to have the most, and fastest, correct guesses.

These days, largely as a result of various television programs, such as *Give Us A Clue* in the UK and *Celebrity Charades* in the US, various recognized signs are allowed to indicate how many words, how many syllables, short words, whether the whole is a book, film, song, or something else. In a retro game of Charades, these signals are definite no-nos, so it's more important to decide the rules beforehand, especially what kind of words or phrases are to be allowed—words of two or three syllables, for example, only very well-known phrases, no recent movies—and no pointing to items in the room. It may be harder, but that's the way it was done.

## Dumb Crambo

The rules of Charades are reversed. Players are still divided into two teams. One team (the audience) chooses the word to be guessed and gives the other team (the actors) a rhyming word. The actors have three chances to act out what they think the word is. If they don't get it right, or their acting is not good enough for the audience to understand what they're miming, they lose. If you're scoring, the audience gets the point! Crambo, also known as Capping the Rhyme, is the speaking version. A similar game, called the ABC of Aristotle, may have been played in England as long ago as the fourteenth century.

# I Spy with My Little Eye

This was apparently recognized as a game coming on for a hundred years ago, although who can say whether similar guessing games haven't existed for a lot longer than that. When didn't those in charge of young children cast around to find ways of entertaining them quietly? This one seems fairly obvious but perhaps that's because it has become so familiar.

One person chooses an item that he can see and says: "I spy with my little eye something beginning with B," or whatever the first letter may be, and everyone else takes turns to guess what it is. One variant for younger children is to use colors, so that it becomes, "I spy with my little eye something yellow," for instance. Children can be very imaginative when it comes to choosing what everyone else has to guess. When I played the game with my young nephew some years ago, he fooled the assembled grown-ups with "I spy with my little eye something beginning with R." Answer: "Reflection." We were sitting near a mirror.

## I'm thinking of...

This is a variant of I Spy with My Little Eye, but you don't actually have to spy anything—you just have to see it in your mind's eye. To give the others a fighting chance, beside giving the first letter, you could say that you're thinking of a flower or whatever it might be. The same principle can be applied to Hide and Seek—you pretend you're hiding in a specific place and everyone else has to guess where it is. Again, you could nudge them in the right direction by saying whether it's indoors or out—or not, if you want to string it all out a bit.

# Twenty Questions

All the rage in Victorian times, Twenty Questions was created in America and is one of those straightforward games that just finds its way into the human psyche! Somebody thinks of a place, person, or object and the others have to guess what it is by asking questions the answers to which are either "Yes" or "No." These days, it's acceptable to agree beforehand if "Possibly," "Kind of," and "Sometimes" are to be allowed, but originally those answers were strictly off limits, resulting in a forfeit (see page 28). Any intermediate guess is counted as a question. Whoever gets it right is the next one to think of a subject. If everyone is stumped, the winner gets to think, and answer, again.

"It was a Game called Yes and No, where Scrooge's nephew had to think of something, and the rest must find out what; he only answering to their questions yes or no, as the case was."

Charles Dickens, *A Christmas Carol* (1843)

The Ghost of Christmas Present takes Scrooge to the party during old Ebeneezer's journey toward abandoning "Bah! Humbug!" in favor of "A Merry Christmas to you!" Once he gets there under his own steam, far from being the "something" that his nephew had thought up (identified as an animal like a bear with a sore head), good old Scrooge revels in a "Wonderful party, wonderful games, wonderful unanimity, won-der-ful happiness!" What a lot games can do!

So popular was Twenty Questions that it was turned into successful radio and television programs on both sides of the Atlantic in the 1940s and 1950s. The original US radio program was broadcast from the Longacre Theatre in New York and listeners were invited to send in subjects for the panelists to guess. The subject most often suggested (allegedly)? Winston Churchill's cigar.

# Animal, Vegetable, or Mineral?

In a variant of Twenty Questions, subjects are divided into these categories, so the first question is usually, "Is it animal?" The classification is necessarily very wide—anything derived from an animal or from plant material, such as a leather bag or a book, is "animal" or "vegetable;" anything else is "mineral." If an object combines two or all three, choose the predominant one.

This was a parlor game in the early twentieth century. One side would decide on the subject and the other would ask the questions in turn. Answers were confined to "Yes" or "No"—a "Maybe" or a "Not sure" generated a forfeit (see page 28).

In the 1950s, the BBC made a version of an American TV show, "What in the World?", calling it "Animal, Vegetable, Mineral?" Archaeologists, naturalists, and other academics were asked to identify various historical artifacts.

"As boys, when they play at 'how many,' hold out their hands in such a way that, having few, they pretend to have many, and having many, they make believe to have few."

Xenophon (430–354 BCE) *Treatise on the Duties of a Cavalry Officer*

The game of How Many? played in the time of Xenophon is the same as Hul Gul (which is a wonderful name but goodness knows where it comes from). So, an old, old game, and a universal tactic that transcends the years.

# Hul Gul

All you need for this ancient game are some counters—
these could be buttons, marbles, nuts, dried beans, or
anything else suitable. The children take some each, but
make sure no one can see how many they have in their
hand. Then they stand in a circle and one asks his left-
hand neighbor to guess how many counters he is holding.
In another version, the children mill around until one takes
the lead, thrusting out his closed hand and asking the
question of someone else in the group.

The dialogue is quite formal: "Hul Gul," he says (quite
why is not clear) to which the response is, "Hands full."
The first one then says, "Parcel, how many?" If the
second child guesses wrongly (and it would be quite
surprising if he got it right!), he has to give the first one
the difference—if the guess is three and the first child
has five, the second one has to hand over two. The
player who collects the most counters is the winner.

## Odd or Even

A very similar idea to Hul Gul, this game was also played in ancient
times. Instead of guessing the exact number of counters, you just have
to guess whether the number is odd or even. If the guess is right, you
take all the other player's counters. If wrong, you hand over one of your
counters. Whoever collects all the counters wins the game.

# WORD GAMES

Simple word games can easily be adapted to make them more complicated, depending on who's playing. In I Have a Basket, for example, everyone in turn has to say what to put in it, the first thing starting with A, the next one B, and so on. If you have to remember what's been said before, that turns it into a slightly more challenging memory game, often called When I Went Shopping, I Bought ... See how far you can get before your mind goes blank! Everyone else will be sure to remind you after you've been counted out. Tongue Twisters are usually impossible for all but the specially trained—actors, for example. You can make a game out of them by seeing who gets furthest before gobbledegook takes over.

# Tongue twisters

So the sixth sheikh's sixth sheep's sick? Spread the news as fast as you can. How many times can you spit it out before lapsing into total incoherence? Aren't Tongue Twisters great! Young kids especially like them when grown-ups get into a muddle.

No doubt sentences and phrases that are hard to get your tongue around have been a source of amusement for a very long time, although as far as I can discover they've been recorded only in the last few hundred years. Interestingly, two of the best known may well have been based on actual people. In 1770, Pierre Poivre (Peter Pepper), French colonial administrator and horticulturalist, founded the Pamplemousses Botanical Garden in Mauritius, where he grew cloves and nutmeg among many other things, having allegedly obtained them by devious means from the Spice Islands, which were strictly controlled by the Dutch. He became famous for his spicy garden. Pepper in Latin is *piper nigrum* and the Old English for pepper is "pipor"—all coincidence, possibly, but the connection is hard to resist.

Peter Piper picked a peck of pickled peppers.

A peck of pickled peppers Peter Piper picked.

If Peter Piper picked a peck of pickled peppers,

Where's the peck of pickled peppers Peter Piper picked?

First published in *Peter Piper's Practical Principles of Plain and Perfect Pronunciation* in 1813, although according to *The Oxford Companion to Children's Literature* (1984), it may have been well known for some years by then.

Mary Anning was the greatest fossil hunter ever known, according to the Natural History Museum in London. Born into a poor family, she lived all her life in Lyme Regis on England's Jurassic coast, and was taught to look for fossils by her father. They sold their finds to the multitude of tourists who came to visit Lyme Regis in the summer. In 1811, Mary uncovered the skeleton of what was later named an Ichthyosaurus, which was sensational news at the time. She went on to make many more important discoveries and became well respected by the scientific community. It's not to hard to see why many people think that Mary Anning is the "she" who sold seashells on the seashore.

PARLOR GAMES

She sells sea-shells on the sea-shore.

The shells she sells are sea-shells, I'm sure.

For if she sells sea-shells on the sea-shore

Then I'm sure she sells sea-shore shells.

Lyrics by Terry Sullivan, music by Harry Gifford, sung by
Wilkie Bard in the show "Dick Whittington and His Cat" at
Drury Lane Theatre, London, in 1908.

# Alphabet games

A number of word games rely on players being able to come up with answers focused around specific letters. They all make you think!

## Taboo

The aim of this game is to avoid using a certain letter when answering questions. Choose someone to do the answering and the letter to be avoided. Everyone else then asks the chosen one questions, all designed, of course, to make her use the forbidden letter. When she succumbs, choose another letter and let another player have a turn. To make it more difficult, make it a rule that the answers have to be in sentences—it's quite hard to compose a sentence quickly without using a designated letter in it anywhere. Have a go!

## Cupid's Coming

"How is he coming?" "By C." Then everyone in turn has to think of a word beginning with C to describe by what means Cupid is about to arrive—carriage, car, caravan, cart, and so on. Anyone who can't think of a suitable word either has to pay a forfeit (see page 28) or is out. In another version, each person has to think of a relevant verb ending in "ing" to describe the imminent arrival—flying would be appropriate!

Children in New England called the game Comes, It Comes, according to William Newell in *Games and Songs of American Children* (1884): "One child of the party says to another, 'It comes, it comes.' The player addressed replies, 'What do you come by?' The first replies by naming the initial letter of some object in the room; if, for instance, it is the table he has in mind, he says, 'I come by T.' The rest must now guess what thing, beginning with this letter, is meant." Well, I've heard of a flying carpet as a means of transport, but a table? Imaginative kids in New England!

## I Apprenticed My Son

You apprentice your son to a trade and suggest the first thing he has to do begins with a certain letter. Everyone in turn has to guess what it is, just one guess each. The example given in *My Book of Indoor Games* (1916) by Clarence Squareman is "I apprenticed my son to a greengrocer and the first thing he sold was an A."

Not apple, almond, or asparagus—artichoke was the answer. Whoever gets it right is next to apprentice their son. If no one gets it right, you have another turn.

## The Traveler's Alphabet

First, inform the assembled company that you are going somewhere far away beginning with an A—Athens, Amsterdam, Algiers, Albuquerque, Atlanta—wherever takes your fancy. Somewhere exotic adds to the fun.

"What will you do there?" your neighbor asks, and all the words of your reply must begin with an A: "Attend An Acting Academy, Actually," for example. The next player goes somewhere beginning with a B, the next one hightails it off to a C and so on. A mistake means a forfeit (see page 26).

## Our Old Granny Doesn't Like Tea

"What can you give her instead?" you ask and everyone must answer in turn, coming up with an alternative food or drink before the count of five. "Coffee," someone may say—right answer. "Chocolate," another may suggest—wrong answer. Whoever said it must pay a forfeit (see page 26). The trick is no answer must include the letter T. Even when astute kids have cottoned on to this, it's still easy to slip up.

# Consequences

This has apparently been around for many years—referred to as "a very old favorite" that "has lost none of its charms with age" in *My Book of Indoor Games* (1916)—but concrete information on its origins, as far as I can see, is non-existent! No matter. Here's how to play.

Everyone has a sheet of paper and writes down a response to a set list of categories. After each one, the paper is folded over and handed on to the next person, who mustn't look at what the previous person has written. Everyone is writing their own story, but by passing on the sheets the stories are all muddled up. So when each sheet is read out at the end, the tale that emerges is often very funny.

The category list to follow is:
1) one or two adjectives
2) man's name
3) one or two adjectives
4) woman's name
5) where they met
6) what he gave to her
7) what he said to her
8) what she said to him
9) what the consequence was
10) what the world said about it

*For example:* Grumpy Christopher met frivolous Mary at the playground. He gave her his homework to do and said "Have you got a sandwich?" She said to him, "Button it, Buster!" The consequence was the skipping rope broke and they never spoke to each other again, and the world said, "Well, what did you expect?"

Lost and Found follows the same principle but the entries are different:
1) what has been lost
2) by whom
3) at what time
4) where
5) found by
6) in what condition
7) at what time
8) and the reward was

# Birds, Beasts, and Fishes

This is another pencil and paper game. Think of a bird, animal, or fish, and write down the first and last letter, putting crosses to indicate those missed out. To play fair, you should identify the category. For example, say you are thinking of an animal and write down: Exxxxxxt. The others have to guess what it is. Whoever guesses correctly (elephant, in this case) takes the next turn. If they all give up, you have another go.

I remember playing a game with a very similar name as a child—Bird, Beast, and Flower—but the rules were quite different. You had a list of categories—bird, animal, flower, fish, river, town, country, capital city—and, in ten minutes, had to write down an answer next to each one, all beginning with B or whatever the selected letter might be. Then you compared answers, scoring two if no one else had thought of the same answer and one if they had—providing the answer was right, of course.

# Cross Questions and Crooked Answers

To play this game, the children must be able to whisper to their neighbor easily, so sitting in a circle is best. The one to start whispers a question, such as "Do you like apples?" and her neighbor responds with something like, "Yes, when they're crisp and crunchy." Then the neighbor asks her neighbor a different question, "Do you like going to the beach?" for example, and the answer may be "Yes, but only when the sun shines." So it goes on around the circle and each player must remember the question she was asked and also the answer she was given to her own question. The player who went first has to hang on to the answer she was given so she can put it with the question she is asked at the end of the round, when each player repeats what she remembers: "I was asked 'Do you like apples?' and had the answer, 'Yes, but only when the sun shines.'" With luck, the first player will have been asked something like "Do you like snails?" which would go so well with, "Yes, when they're crisp and crunchy." You get the idea!

# Bachelor's Kitchen

One player asks all the others in turn what they will contribute to the bachelor's kitchen. (It doesn't actually matter whose kitchen it is, so the title of the game seems to suggest that years ago bachelors were unlikely to have a fully equipped kitchen! I wonder if that was really so.) Each player offers one item—a saucepan, wooden spoon, doormat, mousetrap, whatever he can think of. It's best if an item is not repeated. When everyone has come up with something that the kitchen can't do without, the questioner's task is to make the players laugh. In pursuit of that admirable aim, he asks each one in turn all sorts of questions to which the response must be exactly the answer given before—no more, no less. "What do you wear on your head?" "A saucepan." "What do you put on your feet?" "A saucepan." And so it goes on until the kid in question can no longer keep a straight face, or until the questioner gives him up as too difficult to crack! Forfeits (see page 26) are the penalty for laughter.

# TABLETOP GAMES

What a blessing are tabletop games—a failsafe way of inducing kids to sit down and play rather than rushing around disturbing the peace and causing mayhem! Of course, they may still be noisy—has anyone ever witnessed a quiet game of Snap?—but at least they're all in one place! Anyway, it can be fun to join in.

> "Do not keep children to their studies by compulsion but by play."
>
> Plato (424/423–348/347 BCE), philosopher

## Cards

Playing cards were "an invention of the devil" according to one John Northbrooke in 1579, no doubt having witnessed a plethora of adult gambling. Actually, they were an invention of the Chinese way back, but the standard deck we know today, which so upset John Northbrooke, originated from France. As time passed, attitudes changed and come the nineteenth and twentieth centuries, card games for children were commonplace. As well as entertainment, they were thought of as an educational tool, teaching children the rudiments of arithmetic as well as social skills, such as taking turns and playing fair.

Snap and Animal Grab fulfilled the top criteria of being fast and noisy and so remain perennially popular among children. They were, and still are, basically the same game, involving dividing the cards as equally as possible among the number of people playing, turning over the top card on your pile when it's your go, and shouting at the top of your voice when it matches another player's card. Snap is usually played with a standard deck while Animal Grab has a pack of specially designed cards, and instead of yelling "Snap" as loudly as your lungs allow, you make the relevant animal noise. So if you turn up a duck and your neighbor already

## Jokers and squeezers

The Joker made its appearance in 1857 and is an American invention, apparently based on the Fool from an original French Tarot deck. It was devised for use in the game of Euchre, which spread from Europe to America after the Revolutionary War (1775–1783).

Shortly afterward, in 1876, the New York Consolidated Card Company included small numbers in the corners of playing cards for the first time, referring to them as squeezers (players could hold cards closer together and still identify what they had in their hands). This idea caught on and other manufacturers in America and Britain quickly followed suit. Up until then, the court cards had been King, Queen, and Knave, but to avoid having two Ks, the Knave became the Jack— the name taken from an English card game (All Fours) played by those lower down the social scale and previously thought too vulgar to use. Practicality took over, however, and J it was.

has said bird on show, you yell "Quack, quack" and grab his pile before he can do the same to you. Old packs of Animal Grab are beautifully illustrated and include the oddity of pigs going "Tig, tig." What was wrong with "Oink, oink?"

Other popular games with designated packs of cards, which are still available, include Happy Families, in which various occupations are represented and you have to collect the four members of the family—Mr Bun the Baker, Mrs Bun the Baker's Wife, Miss Bun the Baker's Daughter, and Master Bun the Baker's Son, for example—by asking the player on your left if he has a particular card that you want for your set. If he has, he must give it to you and you ask again until the answer's "no". Then it's your neighbor's turn. The original 1851 edition (published by John Jaques of London) had 11 families, including Mr Mug the Milkman and Mr Grits the Grocer. You can play more or less the same game with a standard deck, when it's called Go Fish.

You can also play another vintage game, Old Maid, with a standard deck by removing all but one of the Queens. Once the cards are dealt, you discard any pairs you may have and then the dealer offers his hand, face down, to the player on his left, who takes one. If that matches a card he already has, that's another pair to be discarded, and so play progresses until only the Queen is left—referred to, rather cruelly, as the Old Maid. Whoever is left holding her loses the game.

" 'What do you play, boy?' asked Estella of myself, with the greatest disdain.

'Nothing but beggar my neighbour, miss.'

'Beggar him,' said Miss Havisham to Estella. So we sat down to cards …

'He calls the knaves, Jacks, this boy!' said Estella with disdain, before our first game was out. 'And what coarse hands he has! And what thick boots!'

… She won the game, and I dealt. I misdealt, as was only natural, when I knew she was lying in wait for me to do wrong; and she denounced me for a stupid, clumsy laboring-boy."

Charles Dickens, *Great Expectations* (1861)

Poor Pip! Poor Estella, so full of disdain! Beggar My Neighbor (also known as Beat Your Neighbor Out of Doors for some reason) is a simple game—cards are divided equally and each player in turn places one, face up, on a central pile until a picture card or an Ace appears. Then the next player has to add a specific number of cards (one for a Jack, two for a Queen, three for a King, four for an Ace). If that requirement is completed, the player who laid the court card or Ace claims the whole pile and adds it to his own. But while the extra cards are being laid, another picture card or Ace may appear, in which case it takes precedence, so the next player has to add the extra cards, and so it goes on—and it can go on and on and on! The object is to end up with all the cards.

# Dominoes

This childhood favorite has a long but uncertain ancestry. Origins of games using dice or tiles are lost in the dim and distant past, but it's quite possible that Dominoes evolved from them, maybe in China, more than a thousand years ago. They first appeared in Britain via Italy and France in the late eighteenth century, and quickly spread to America, where they were adopted with particular enthusiasm in the south. Dominoes is still regarded as a national game in many parts of the Caribbean. None of this was just for children, of course. As is so often the case, the popularity of Dominoes spread so far and so fast because they were taken up by adults.

In the old days, domino tiles were made of bone and so were white with black spots. Some were made with the tagua nut (known as vegetable ivory). In the early part of the twentieth century they were often made from Bakelite. These days it's more likely to be plastic or wood. Sets usually comprised twenty-eight pieces, each one divided into two by a line across the center, and each one bearing a unique combination of dots, running from blank to six on each end. The double six was the highest value tile. These days, it's possible to find sets with more tiles and more dots, used for more complex games.

## Fives and Threes

This version makes Dominoes more interesting, and is not difficult for kids, especially if they've been paying attention in arithmetic classes. When you lay down a tile, the combination of dots at each end of the line must be divisible by five or three and you score accordingly. For example, if the dots add up to six, you score two because three goes into six twice. If the dots add up to fifteen, you've hit the jackpot since that generates the highest possible score, eight (fifteen is divisible by both five and three). If you don't have a suitable tile, you still take your turn but don't score. That's it. In adult versions, scoring becomes a tad more complicated.

# How to play Dominoes

Several different games were, and still are, played but all of them follow the same basic formula of placing tiles with matching halves together. This is a traditional version for two players, although more can play by each one selecting fewer than seven dominoes to start with.

- Lay all the tiles face down and shuffle them around.

- Both players pick a tile and whoever chooses the one with the most dots goes first.

- Replace the two dominoes, reshuffle, and select seven each, leaving fourteen. Place each one upright in front of you so that your opponent can't see them.

- Whoever is going first lays down the double six if he has it. If not, he should lay another double, but if he doesn't have one, any other domino that he chooses.

- Player two puts down a tile with a matching number of dots on one end lengthwise against the first one.

- Player one does the same, matching a tile at one end of the line or the other, whichever he chooses. Doubles should be placed crosswise. And so the line continues to grow as the game progresses.

- If you can't go, you take a domino from the pool of fourteen until two are left. After that you miss a go.

- When one player has no dominoes left, that round is over. The number of dots on the dominoes the losing player has left are added up and credited to the winning player.

- If neither of you can go, you both add up the dots on your remaining dominoes, the lower number is taken from the higher number and credited to the player with the lower number. The one to make 100 first is the winner.

# Tiddlywinks

What is it about Tiddlywinks, or Tiddledy Winks as it was originally known? How come it brings a smile to the face of kids and grown-ups alike? Invented in England in 1889, by Joseph Fincher, it attained instant craze status and became so popular with adults, on both sides of the Atlantic, that the kids hardly got a look in. Inevitably, the grown-ups moved on to something a little more challenging than flicking a wink into a cup, although it took a decade or so, and left the kids to it.

Players were allocated a number of colored discs (winks), which they had to flip, one at a time, into a target cup by means of pressing another disc, or shooter (these days, delightfully named a squidger), onto each one's rim. If their wink landed on another player's wink, which in those days they were not supposed to do deliberately, that disc was out of play (these days known as squopped.) Fabulous that such Dickensian terms have been adopted in the twenty-first century!

Grown-ups couldn't resist the game's allure, though, and came back to it in a big way in the 1950s, in the wake of a strong revival at the University of Cambridge in England. Now there are numerous clubs and tournaments run by the two national associations—the English Tiddlywinks Association and the North American Tiddlywinks Association. The basic rules haven't changed much, although the undergraduates just had to tinker with them, naturally, and so the adult game has became a lot more complex. Good luck to them. The kids know how to play their own game and that's really all that matters.

> "Even in the matter of nursery games the Victorian child took things very seriously. There were some board games, however, which provided little or no intellectual stimulus. Chief among these was … tiddlywinks, whose apparent inanity (to the uninitiated) is often regarded as the ultimate in useless activities."

James A. Mackay, *Childhood Antiques* (1976)
No undercover educational tool this. No wonder it was a big hit—bring it on!

## Anyone for tennis?

In light of the success of Tiddledy Winks, games manufacturers fell over themselves to create new and improved versions. E.I. Horsman was first in 1890 when he brought out Tiddledy Winks Tennis, which appears to have been the big hit of that year's Christmas season. According to *The American Stationer* "… [Mr Horsman] thinks there will be no rest for him until every man, woman and child in the United States has one" —not that he was complaining. In fact, he was probably laughing all the way to the bank. This success generated all sorts of variations including Basketball, Croquet, and Golf Tiddlywinks.

# BOARD GAMES

Ancient civilizations produced some amazing innovators and whoever created the very first games to use the equivalent of a board, separate pieces, and possibly some means of determining number of moves, were right up there among the best.

The oldest board games to have been discovered—Senet, the Royal Game of Ur, and Mancala-type games in the Middle East, Weiqi in China, later known as Go in Japan, Pachisi, Chaupar, and Chaturanga (forerunner of Chess) in India, and the strategic Tafl games of northern Europe among them—were sophisticated and challenging in varying degrees. Whether children got in on the act back then is open to conjecture, but kids are always innovators in their own way, too, so maybe they devised their own versions. It wouldn't be surprising.

However that was thousands of years ago. Retro board games from the eighteenth, nineteenth, and early twentieth centuries were mostly originally for adults but hijacked by kids, so all generations could play, separately or together. One exception is Chutes and Ladders, which was always supposed to be a means of teaching children right from wrong.

Other board games of the era continued along that same path of righteousness. In The Mansion of Happiness (1843) you reached Heaven if you were good and managed to avoid the pitfalls of audacity, cruelty, immodesty, and ingratitude. They led only to misery and poverty. Within a few decades, though, the idea of money bringing happiness had filtered through and in The Checkered Game of Life (1860—revised as The Game of Life in 1960), participants went to college and pursued success. Shockingly, there was a square for suicide—if you landed on that, you were most definitely out! In the Game of the District Messenger Boy (1886) you started at the bottom and ended up running the company.

Ideal family entertainment, equally absorbing for young and old—no wonder the whole idea of board games has survived for millennia.

## Old favorites

The Landlord's Game, created by Elizabeth Magie, was patented in 1904 and sold in America between 1910 and 1939 and in Britain from 1913 under the title Brer Fox an' Brer Rabbit. In 1935, Ms Magie sold the patent to Parker Brothers, who had acquired the rights to a similar game, Monopoly. Some corporate shenanigans and a few law suits later, it seems that Monopoly may well have been derived from The Landlord's Game—ironic really when you think that the original was anti "land-grabbing" and Monopoly encourages players to buy up as much as possible.

Alfred M. Butts invented a word game, Lexiko, in 1931, modified it as Criss-Crosswords in 1938, and in the face of general indifference, sold the rights to James Brunot in 1948. Brunot tinkered with the rules, changed the name to Scrabble, manufactured a couple of thousand sets and lost money. Then chance took a hand. The story goes that in 1952 Jack Strauss came across the game while on vacation. He just happened to be the president of Macy's at the time, and when he discovered his store didn't stock the game, he placed a large order. The rest, as they say, is history.

# Chutes and Ladders/ Snakes and Ladders

"England's famous indoor sport" games manufacturers Milton Bradley called it when introducing their version to America in 1943 under the name of Chutes and Ladders. To be more accurate, they should have referred to it as India's famous game because that's where it originated, although no one knows exactly when—possibly as early as the second century BCE but certainly by the 1200s. Mokshapat, or Moksha Patamu (Leela in the Jain version), was an effective lesson in morality for children, emphasizing the infinitely preferable consequences of living a good life rather than a bad one. The ladders represented virtues and by climbing them you could reach salvation (Moksha) at the top of the board; but it was all too easy to slide down the snakes, vices that took you to a much worse place—and there were more snakes than ladders.

This high moral tone must have appealed to the nineteenth century Brits in India, because they brought it back with them and it went down a storm in Victorian England. The first boards were Indian in design, and there were as many ladders as snakes, but it wasn't long before various other versions appeared—one where you finished in the middle rather than at the top, one that abandoned the virtues and vices theme and featured hitting winning shots in golf, cricket, and soccer.

By the time Milton Bradley cottoned on to the game's potential, the Indian connection had all but disappeared, although the good and evil theme survived. Climbing the ladder was the reward for good behavior, sliding down the chute was just the opposite, although in real life, isn't sliding down more fun than climbing up? Be that as it may, new editions of this perennial survivor are easily available, while older ones can be found by scouring the internet, and possibly thrift stores.

> "All games have morals; and the game of Snakes and Ladders captures, as no other activity can hope to do, the eternal truth that for every ladder you climb, a snake is waiting just around the corner; and for every snake, a ladder will compensate."
>
> Salman Rushdie (b. 1947), novelist

## How to play

You need a board, counters, a spinner or dice, and at least two players. The board, liberally covered with chutes (or snakes) and ladders, is divided into numbered squares, usually starting with 1 at bottom left and progressing in rows to 100 at the top. Players move by spinning the spinner or throwing the dice. If you land on a square where a ladder starts, up you go to the square where it ends. If you land on a square with the top of a chute (or where that old snake is resting his sneaky head), down you slide. So you either skip a lot of squares or have to go through them again, depending on the luck of the spin or throw—a six gets you another turn. The winner is the first one to the top, and just to add a bit of spice, you have to get the exact number to land on the winning square or miss a turn.

# Parcheesi/Ludo

An ancient cross and circle game from India, Pachisi, is the forerunner of this stalwart of the games' shelf. A slightly more complicated version, Chaupar, was a favorite of the sixteenth century Mogul emperor Akbar, who had giant courts of inlaid marble built in his palaces at Agra and Allahabad and used slaves from the harem as counter pieces.

In the early 1860s, games manufacturer Jaques and Sons produced an English version of the game, calling it Patchesi, but in 1896 they simplified the rules, making it much more of a children's game, and changed the name to Ludo (Latin for "I play"). Meantime, the game had crossed the Atlantic and in 1874 it was trademarked in America as Parcheesi and since then has gone from strength to strength, becoming one of America's longest-selling games—best-selling, too, until Monopoly came along and raced to the number-one spot, seemingly forever!

The traditional game of Pachisi/Chaupar, which is still played in India, uses an embroidered cloth cross shape with a square in its center. The Parcheesi/Ludo board is based on this and hasn't changed much in the last hundred or so years. Neither have the rules. The idea is to be the first to race all your pieces around the board into the center square. A few obstructions may occur on the way, depending on other players' moves. A throw of the dice, rather than the small cowrie shells of the Indian game, determines how many spaces may be moved.

## Sorry!

William Henry Storey's new board game came on the market in the early 1930s and has never been away. Also based on Pachisi, it is slightly more complicated than Parcheesi/Ludo, but is still a great game for kids from the age of about six up. The aim is to get your four pieces around the board to your home base before anyone else beats you to it. Moves are made by turning cards rather than throwing dice, and you can dislodge other players' pieces, sending them back to the start, introducing children to the idea of tactical play.

## A game of many names

Selchow & Righter owned the copyright of the name Parcheesi, but that didn't stop McLouglins or Milton Bradley jumping on the bandwagon—they merely called their games India and The Game of India. In 1915, Parker Brothers brought out Pollyanna, a similar game based on the novel by Eleanor Porter, which they continued to produce in various guises—including The Glad Game, Dixie, and The Popular Game of Broadway—until 1967. In the long run, it didn't matter—all four firms were taken over by Hasbro, who still sell Parcheesi, with ongoing success.

## Backgammon

A century or so ago, before the doubling strategy revitalized the game as a gambler's dream, Backgammon was often played by children. For most of its history, though, it has been a gambling game. The earliest reference to it is in the *Oxford English Dictionary* of 1645, but the game is much older than that. Some say its origins lie in ancient Egypt, or earlier, others that it can be traced back to Pachisi (see page 132). No one knows for certain. It is true that the Romans played it. They called it *Tabulae* (Tables)

and *Ludus Duodecim Scriptorum* (the twelve-line game). The Emperor Claudius had a board built into his chariot, to help while away the time on his travels. It became so popular in Europe that it was banned several times—the Church disapproved of any games that could conceivably involve gambling—so folk would disguise the board and pieces as books! Backgammon has been played in America since the seventeenth century. Thomas Jefferson was an enthusiast, apparently taking time out from drafting the Declaration of Independence in 1776 to play—perhaps it provided some necessary light relief from such weighty business.

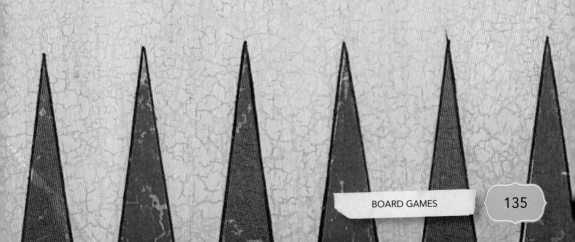

# Checkers/Draughts

Ostensibly more straightforward than chess, Checkers/Draughts is a game for all ages, as simple or complex as two evenly matched players care to make it. The basic rules haven't changed over the years, so kids can pit their wits against grandparents, who probably did much the same with their grandparents when they were young.

The game is played on the same checkered board as Chess, usually eight squares by eight. Each player has 12 round pieces, or draughts, and whoever claims the black set always begins the game. The idea is to prevent your opponent from being able to move when it's his turn, either because you've blocked him in or because you've cunningly captured all his pieces, removing them from play. You do this by moving one piece at a time toward the other end of the board, from black square to black square only, and jumping over the opposition into an empty square whenever you can—a piece jumped is a piece captured —but just one at a time. Once you reach your opponent's back line with one of your pieces, it is transformed into a king (doubling up with a previously captured piece) and a king has the freedom of the board, more or less. It can be moved backward as well as forward and jump several opposing pieces in the same turn. So the more the better!

Around a thousand years ago, when the ancient Egyptian board game of Alquerque, or Qirkat, was already old hat, someone in France had the bright idea of adapting it to play on a Chess board with 12 pieces. Several rule changes later, Draughts had become popular all over Europe. Books were written about it, and by the eighteenth century it had infiltrated America as Checkers and become entrenched in the American way of life.

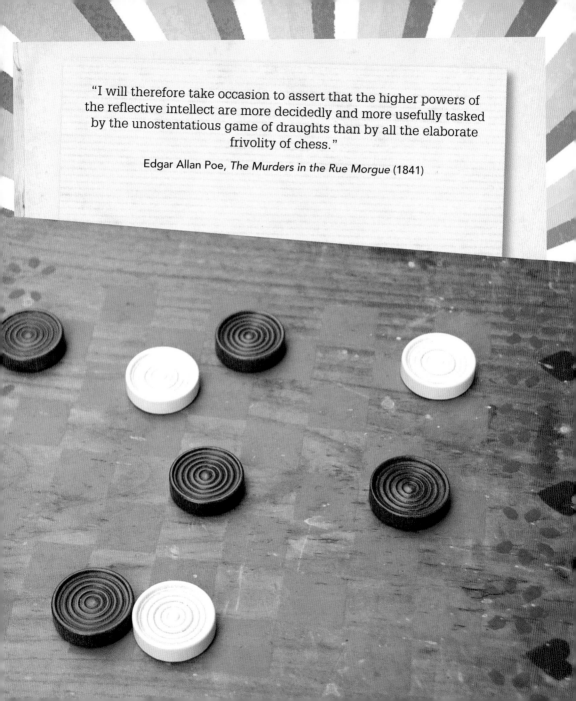

"I will therefore take occasion to assert that the higher powers of the reflective intellect are more decidedly and more usefully tasked by the unostentatious game of draughts than by all the elaborate frivolity of chess."

Edgar Allan Poe, *The Murders in the Rue Morgue* (1841)

# Chinese Checkers

In this case, the clue is not in the name. The game of Chinese Checkers was invented in Germany in 1892 and has nothing to do with China, Checkers, or Draughts. Originally called Stern-Halma ("stern" is the German word for "star") it is very like the slightly older game of Halma but played on a six-pointed, star-shaped board with either pegs or marbles as pieces. Each star is a home base and players have to move their ten pegs, or marbles, each set differently colored, to the star opposite, either one space at a time or by jumping over an opponent's peg into an empty space. It was introduced in England, probably as Star-Halma, in 1909.

It came to in America in 1928, snappily named Hop Ching Checker Game, but fortunately its publishers, J. Pressman & Co, dreamed up its more familiar name shortly afterward. The fad for Mahjong was in full swing so maybe a Chinese name seemed appropriate at the time. As a marketing ploy it certainly worked—the 1930s was the era of Chinese Checkers. Simple enough for young children to play, either with each other or with grown-ups, it has survived unchanged as a real family board game.

## Halma

American surgeon Dr George Howard Monks created Halma (Greek for "jump") sometime between 1883 and 1884, inspired by a now obscure English game, Hoppity, as reported to him by his brother Robert, who was in England at that time. The game is played on a square board and four sets of playing pieces are supplied, each one differently colored. Rather oddly, two sets have thirteen pieces and two have nineteen pieces. Two, three or four people may play and the object is to move all your pieces from your home corner to the opposite corner, by moving one space at a time or by jumping over other pieces, often in a chain.

It was a big hit in Victorian Britain as well as in America, but seems to have been overtaken in both countries by Chinese Checkers, which has a smaller board and is quicker to play.

# RESOURCES

Memories of childhood antics came flooding back in researching and writing this book. Memories, however, can be notoriously unreliable, and the way games were played in my London suburban neighborhood was probably not the way they were played elsewhere. So I scoured the internet for information and found plenty of it, for which I'm duly grateful. The following books and websites were especially helpful:

*Games and Songs of American Children* William Wells Newell (1884)
*Sports and Pastimes of the People of England* Joseph Strutt (1801)
*The Traditional Games of England, Scotland and Ireland* Alice Bertha Gomme (published in two volumes, 1894 and 1898)
*My Book of Indoor Games* Clarence Squareman (1916)
*Entertaining Made Easy* Emily Rose Burt (1919)

You can find out-of-print books on several websites, including gutenberg.org

americantoymarbles.com
classicgamesandpuzzles.com
collectorsweekly.com/cards/playing-cards
domino-games.com/domino-history.html
domino-play.com
marblecollecting.com
newyorkstreetgames.com
  (New York Street Games is a documentary
  available on dvd; see the synopsis on
  Wikipedia)
streetplay.com
tradgames.org.uk
victorianchildren.org
victorianschool.co.uk
wopc.co.uk/usa  (World of Playing Cards)

Websites that offer old-fashioned
toys and games for sale include:

antiquetoychest.com
fairetymetoys.com
games-collector.com
historicgames.com
houseofmarbles.com
jaqueslondon.co.uk
mastersgames.com
ohsayusa.com
tintoyarcade.com
traditionalgardengames.com

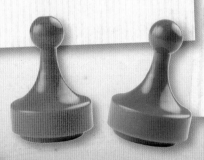

# Index

1, 2, 3, O'Leary  65

alphabet games  116–17
Animal, Vegetable or Mineral?
    110
Anning, Mary  114–15
Ante Over  67
arch games  74, 80–1

babies, games with  23
Bachelor's Kitchen  119
Backgammon  134–5
ball games  62–9
    against the wall  64–5
    Balls and Bonnets  65
    Earth, Air, Fire, and Water  79
balloons  79
Barley-Brake  52
baseball  67
Bedlams  56
Birds, Beasts and Fishes  117
Blind Man's Buff  92–3
board games  128–39
British Bulldog  52–3
bubbles, blowing  16, 17
buttons  36–7, 109

calming games  97
Capture the Flag  54–5
card games  120–3
Cat's Cradle  34–5
chairs, changing  78, 94
charades  102–5
chasing games  32, 50–61
Checkers  136–7
Chinese Checkers  138

Chutes and Ladders  130–1
circle games  74–83, 95, 118
computer games  13
Conqueror  47
Consequences  116–17
counting out  24–7, 51
Crack the Whip  34
Cross Questions and Crooked
Answers  118
Cupid's Coming  114

dabs  20
dips  24, 26–7
Do as I do games  86–7
Do You Love Your Neighbor?
    106
dolls  16, 22
dominoes  124–5
Draughts  136–7
Duck on a Rock  60
Dumb Crambo  105

Earth, Air, Fire, and Water  79

figures, paper  22
Five stones  20
Follow My Leader  87
football  62–3
forfeits  28–9, 79, 97
fossils  112–13
Fungo  69

Game of Graces  40–51
games
    development  12–13
    purpose  6–9
Grandmother's Footsteps  85
guessing games  102–9

Halma  139
Hi Spy  58–9
Hide and Seek  32, 88–9
hoop and stick  18, 40
hopscotch  12, 42–5
horses  16, 17, 19

Hot Boiled Beans and Bacon  91
How many miles to Babylon?  53
Hul Gul  109
hula hoop  16
Hunt the Slipper  74
Hunt the Squirrel  76–7
Hunt the Thimble  90

I Apprenticed My Son  115
I Spy with My Little Eye  106
imagination  12, 14–15, 22–3
improvisation  15, 20, 32, 62
Internet websites  141
invention  15, 22, 32
'It', being  24, 51, 58

jacks  20
Jacob's ladder  16
jigsaw puzzles  16
Jokers  121
Judge and Jury  97

Keep Away  66
Keep Ball  66
Kick the Can  58
Kick the Wickey  34
knucklebones  20

Leapfrog  34
London Bridge is Falling Down
    81
Lookabout  90–1

Ludo 132–3
make believe 22–3
marbles 12, 46–9, 109
mechanical toys 19
Monopoly 129
Mother May I? 86
Musical Chairs 94–5

Nine Holes 49
nursery rhymes 23

Odd or Even 109
Oranges and Lemons 80–1
Our Old Granny doesn't like Tea 115
outdoor games 13, 15, 32–69

painting 16
Parcheesi 132–3
parlor games 100–39
    board games 128–39
    card games 120–3
    dominoes 124–5
    guessing games 102–9
    tiddlywinks 126–7
    word games 110–19
party games 72–97
Pass the Parcel 75
pencil and paper games 116–17
Piggy in the Middle 66
Pin the Tail on the Donkey 72–3
playtime 12–15
Pogo sticks 16
Pooh Sticks 33
Prisoner's Base 57
puppets 16

Red Light, Green Light 85
Red Rover 53

Relievo 56
resources 140–1
retro games 12–29
Reverend Crawley's Game 96
rhymes
    ball games 64, 65
    charades 102
    counting-out 24, 26–7
    nursery 23
    party games 80–3
    skipping 39
    tongue twisters 111, 113
Ring Around the Rosie 83
ring games 74–83, 95, 118
Ring a Ring o' Roses 82–3
Ring Taw/Ringers 48
Ringolevio 56–7
roller skates 16
rounders 69
rubber balls 62–3

Sardines 89
scooters 16
Scrabble 129
Sea King 95
searching games 88–93
seats, changing 78, 94
Sheep and Wolf 59
Simon Says 86
singing 23
skipping 38–9
Skyte the Bob 37
Sleeping Lions 97
Snakes and Ladders 130–1
sneaking-up games 84–7
soldiers 22
solitaire 16
space hopper 16
Spaldeen 63

Squeezers 121
Statues 85
Stealing Sticks 55
Stern-Halma 138
Stickball 68–9
street games 15, 32, 56, 62–3

tabletop games 120–39
Taboo 114
tag 51
taw 46, 48
tea parties 22
teddy bears 21
theatres 22
tiddlywinks 126–7
toddlers, games with 23
Tom Tiddler's Ground 61
tongue twisters 111–13
tops 17, 19
toys
    improvised 15, 20, 32
    retro 16–19
Traveler's Alphabet 115
Tug-o'-War 34
Twenty Questions 107–8

Victorian games 18, 26, 28–9, 62, 78, 90, 107, 127, 130, 139

What's the Time, Mr Fox/Wolf? 84
word games 110–19

Yards Off 58

zoetrope 16

# ACKNOWLEDGMENTS

Nostalgia rules OK when it comes to revisiting childhood. I spent some months wallowing in Tag, British Bulldog, Statues, Sorry, Marbles, and all those lovely games that were an integral part of it. It's been enormous fun. What a shame if they fall out of style and today's kids miss out. I hope this book may reinvigorate at least a few of them. So many thanks to Pete at CICO for coming up with the idea and to Cindy for saying yes! Thanks also to Anna for shepherding it along, and for finding such wonderful, eye-catching illustrations, Alice Potter for drawing some specially, Sally for supervising the superb design, and designer Mark Latter for putting it all together so beautifully.

Thanks too, to Rodney, as always, for listening and laughing in the right places.